I0804278

Diary
— of a —
Malcontent

MY EXPERIENCE AS A CIVILIAN EMPLOYEE AT
THE NEW YORK CITY DEPARTMENT OF CORRECTION

STEVE NEWMAN

Diary of a Malcontent: My experience as a civilian employee at the New York City Department of Correction

Cover art by John Tenniel
Book design by The Troy Book Makers

Printed in the United States of America

The Troy Book Makers • Troy, New York • thetroybookmakers.com

To order additional copies of this title, contact your favorite local bookstore or visit www.shoptbmbooks.com

Library of Congress Control Number: 2020914102
ISBN: 978-1-61468-582-1

Dedicated to my wife Barbara, and to her family.

To Rav Yechiel Sitzman, of blessed memory.

TABLE OF CONTENTS

PART ONE: RETALIATION

PART TWO: DISCIPLINARY CHARGES ARE ADJOURNED CONTEMPLATING DISMISSAL

PART THREE: THREE-YEAR CAMPAIGN OF HARASSMENT

PART FOUR: CONSTRUCTIVE DISCHARGE

PART FIVE: TITLE VII AND DISCRIMINATION

PART SIX: SETTLEMENT

PART SEVEN: NOTES

DRAMATIS PERSONAE

Assistant Commissioner
Systems Director, Douglas E. Waldmann
First Executive Director, Bob Creed
Second Executive Director, Raymond Hickox
Third Executive Director
Program Manager
Director of Telecommunications
Inspector General
Deputy Commissioner for Trials
EEO Officer
EEO Director

There was a small city, with few people in it, and a great king came upon it and he surrounded the city with a siege wall. And there was found therein a poor wise man, and he extricated the city through his wisdom, but no man remembered that poor man.

Ecclesiastes.

TIMELINE

January 1990, Interviewed for Civil Service appointment.

February 1990, Appointed to Department of Correction from civil service list.

April 1990, Report to work.

March 1991, Program Manager gave me Visitors Pass assignment.

March 1991, Program Manager gave me satisfactory performance evaluation.

March 1991, Executive Director became sick.

March 1991, New Executive Director appointed.

April 1991, Completed probation.

April 1991, Program Manager reported that I made personal use of the computer.

April 1991, Executive Director Hickox called me obnoxious, revoked Sabbath accommodation and threatened disciplinary charges about Visitors Pass system.

September 1991, Grieved to City Labor Relations Director that Visitors Pass assignment was out of title.

September 1991, Completed the Visitors Pass system.

October 1991, Clocks set for daylight savings.

October 1991, Requested accommodation for Sabbath observance from Executive Director and EEO Officer.

October 1991, Department revoked computer password and served me with disciplinary charges.

October 1991, Submitted Rabbi's letter about Sabbath observance to EEO Officer.

November 1991, Took civil service Computer Specialist Software promotional examination.

November 1991, Complained to the Inspector General for Correction.

November 1991, EEO Officer denied my request to leave at 1:00 pm on Fridays and make up time.

November 1991, Step One Conference.

November 1991, Took sick leave.

December 1991, Complained to City Personnel Director.

December 1991, Complained to EEOC.

January 1992, Meeting with Union psychiatrist.

January 1992, Complained to Deputy Commissioner for Trials.

February 1992, Reported Program Manager's violating residency requirements to Investigation.

February 1992, Complained to my City Council Member.

March 1992, Returned from sick leave.

March 1992, Complained to EEO Director.

May 1992, Complained to City Council President.

May 1992, Mayor appointed new Commissioner for Correction.

May 1992, Department of Investigation investigated residency of Program Manager.

May 1992, Negative performance evaluation recommending termination of employment.

May 1992, Program Manager told me that I am a dead man.

May 1992, Co-worker swore affidavit retracting statement.

June 1992, Commissioner replied to City Council President.

June 1992, State Division of Human Rights found probable cause of discrimination.

June 1992, Executive Director ordered me to report to Systems Director.

June 1992, Assistant Commissioner appointed.

July 1992, Assistant Commissioner set fire to wastepaper basket.

August 1992, Assistant Commissioner disagreed with Rabbi's letter and gave me an IIS assignment.

August 1992, Program Manager resigned.

November 1992, Assistant Commissioner warned me not to tell lies about the Department.

November 1992, Systems Director prohibited me from speaking with co-workers.

January 1993, Executive Director prohibited me from reading newspapers.

February 1993, SDHR vacated probable cause finding and reopened investigation.

February 1993, I asked EEOC to handle investigation.

March 1993, My name not included in list of authorized users of computer passwords.

April 1993, Disciplinary charges adjourned contemplating dismissal.

April 1993, Second Executive Director fired. Third Executive Director appointed.

May 1993, Information Systems Division held party to which I was not invited.

May 1993, Systems Director recommended referring me for psychological evaluation.

May 1993, Systems Director ordered me to report to junior employee.

June 1993, Arbitrator held hearing for out of title grievance.

June 1993, Systems Director Waldmann shouted at me. I complained.

June 1993, Systems Director recommended new disciplinary charges.

July 1993, Assistant Commissioner told Commissioner that he was taking action against me.

July 1993, Negative performance evaluation recommended termination of employment.

July 1993, Systems Director recommended Assistant Commissioner to dismiss me.

July 1993, Arbitrator decided my Visitors Pass system was out of title.

July 1993, Assistant Commissioner transferred me to Personnel.

August 1993, EEOC issued Notice of Right to Sue and closed case.

September 1993, I filed complaint with Federal Court.

December 1993, Sent on two-day Microsoft DOS training course.

February 1994, Awarded Master's degree in Public Administration.

March 1994, Executive Director gave me corrective interview.

January 1995, Assistant Commissioner transferred me to Rikers Island.

January 1995, Telecommunications Director denied me access to a computer.

January 1995, Systems Director denied me training.

January 1995, Telecommunications Director prohibited me from kosher food at jail cafeteria.

February 1995, Telecommunications Director prohibited me from speaking to consultants.

February 1995, Personnel transferred my file to Rikers Island.

February 1995, Found swastika on my desk.

February 1995, Mailed certified delivery letter of resignation.

February 1995, Post Office delivered to me signed dated certified mail receipt.

February 1995, Visited Personnel, handed letter of resignation received receipt.

February 1995, Visited Personnel, handed ID Card and Department Rules, received receipt.

July 1995, Unemployment Benefits Judge held hearing and denied benefits.

November 1996, Passed Computer Specialist Software promotional examination.

March 1997, Unemployment Insurance Appeal Board found that I had good cause to leave my employment.

May 1997, US Senator wrote to Second Circuit to request trial date.

May 1997, New Judge appointed and trial date set.

May 1997, City settled complaint for cash.

LIST OF EXHIBITS

PART ONE

RETALIATION

CHAPTER ONE

HONEYMOON

Oh what a beautiful morning, Oh what a beautiful day.
RODGERS AND HAMMERSTEIN.

These events took place in lower Manhattan during the presidency of Bush the Father; in the days of yore before emails and the internet, and while the old World Trade Center still stood.

The first year ran smoothly. I passed a civil service exam for Computer Associate Software. In February 1990, the Executive Director of the Information Systems Division of the New York City Department of Correction appointed me from the civil service list. In April 1990, I reported for work and I reported directly to the Program Manager. Like all new employees, I attended an orientation course. For the first year, I wrote a series of computer programs used by the Department's Labor Relations unit.

The Executive Director and the Program Manager provided accommodation for me to leave work early at 1:00 pm on Friday afternoons for Sabbath observance and to make up the time.

My father had been a career civil servant. I was proud to be a civil servant and I enrolled at Baruch College CUNY for a Master's degree in Public Administration. The Program Manager wrote a letter recommending me to Baruch College and the College granted me a scholarship.

In March 1991, the Program Manager gave me a satisfactory performance evaluation. In April 1991, I passed my year of probation. But also in March 1991, Bob Creed, the first Executive Director, became sick and, in April 1991, he left the Department. He had interviewed me in 1990 and he had appointed me from the civil service list. Bob Creed had been my friend. Now I was on my own.

In March 1991, a new Executive Director was appointed. His name was Raymond Hickox. The Executive Director assembled us. This was the first time that I ever saw him. He had something very important to say to us and we all gathered around to hear what he would say. He told us that he was going to make changes. A cockroach chose this auspicious moment to scuttle across the room. The Executive Director stomped his foot on the cockroach and then ground it into the floor. The honeymoon was over.

CHAPTER TWO

SABBATH OBSERVANCE

Jewish philosophy compares the Sabbath to a Queen. It compares the arrival of the Sabbath to having a Queen come to visit one's house. When the Queen comes to visit, one prepares in dignity, not in a rush. One prepares the Sabbath meals and there should be a hot, fresh delicious dinner ready to be served at the table. One shaves, showers and wears clean fresh clothes. One lights candles. One does not keep the Queen standing outside waiting. One welcomes the Queen as she arrives.

In April 1990, I started work at the Department. My normal hours of work were, I came to work at 8:00 am, had a one-hour lunch, from 12:00 noon until 1:00 pm, and went home at 4:00 pm. This was called my "tour." At that time, I was living in Washington Heights, in northern Manhattan. My commute home was about one hour.

In October 1990, the clocks were set for daylight savings. The Jewish religion mandates the observance of the Sabbath. During winter, the Sabbath arrived as early as 4:10 pm on Fridays. I needed time to travel home from work and to prepare for the Sabbath. I needed an accommodation by the Department for my Sabbath observance. The Executive Director and the Program Manager agreed to let me rearrange my tour to leave early on Fridays at 1:00 pm for Sabbath observance and to make up the time. These are the details of this accommodation during winter 1990-1991. I came to work at 8:00 am every day. On Mondays, Tuesdays,

Wednesdays and Thursdays, I had a one-hour lunch from 12:00 noon until 1:00 pm. On Mondays and Tuesdays, I went home at 5:00 pm. On Wednesdays and Thursdays, I went home at 4:00 pm. On Fridays, I came to work at 8:00 am, worked straight until 1:00 pm without lunch, and at 1:00 pm I went home.

Two hours were rearranged but the sum total number of hours which I worked during the week were the same. No other employee's working hours needed to be changed for this accommodation and there was no cost to the Department. No one asserted that this accommodation would cause the Department undue hardship. Both the Executive Director and the Program Manager agreed to this arrangement. It was a custom agreed between the three of us but not set down in writing. This is how the Department and its managers had reasonably accommodated my Sabbath observance without undue hardship during the winter of 1990-1991.

In March 1991, Executive Director Bob Creed became sick and, in April 1991, he left the Department. In March 1991, Raymond Hickox was appointed Executive Director; this is he who had stomped upon the cockroach. He replaced Bob Creed.

In April 1991, Executive Director Hickox called me into his office. He told me that I am obnoxious. He canceled the accommodation for Sabbath observance that Bob Creed had approved. He told me that I had to leave at 4:00 pm on Fridays as he did not approve of employees working irregular hours. He threatened to bring me up on disciplinary charges if I did not complete the Visitors Pass system.

In October 1991, the clocks were set for daylight savings. This year, 1991, my need to observe the Sabbath was to become a problem. I was not the only Jew employed at the Department of Correction but I was the only computer programmer in the Department who was Jewish. There were other Jews in the Department besides me but they did not leave early on Friday for Sabbath observance. There was one Jew in the Department who left at 2:00 pm on Fridays to observe the Sabbath. But the Executive Director had told me that I could not leave work until 4:00 pm on Fridays.

I spoke to my supervisor, the Program Manager. He told me that he himself had no objection. He said that it was Systems Director Waldmann who objected to my leaving early on Friday for Sabbath observance. Why would the Systems Director have a problem with my leaving early on Friday for Sabbath observance when the Program Manager, my immediate supervisor, did not have a problem?

On October 4, 1991, I approached Executive Director Hickox to request accommodation to observe the Sabbath. I requested to leave on Friday each week at 1:00 pm and to make up the time on other days. I hoped to obtain the same arrangement in 1991 as I had been granted in 1990. But the Executive Director remained silent and he did not grant my request.

On October 8, 1991, I approached the Department of Correction's Equal Employment Opportunity officer. She met with me straightaway. I told her that I am Jewish, I observe the Jewish religion and I observe the Sabbath. I requested accommodation to observe the Sabbath. I requested to leave on Friday each week at 1:00 pm and to make up the time on other days. No other employee's working hours needed to be changed for this accommodation. I told her that in 1990, the first Executive Director had accommodated my Sabbath observance and he had let me leave at 1:00 pm on Fridays and make up the time. I told the EEO Officer that I had approached the new Executive Director but that he did not respond. I naively expected the EEO Officer to pick up the phone, speak for five minutes with the Executive Director and then tell me that the Department had approved my request. But she remained silent.

I submitted a letter from my Rabbi both to the Executive Director and to the EEO Officer. The letter said that I am a member of the Congregation, I am Jewish, I need to leave work at 1:00 pm on Fridays to observe the Sabbath and I am willing to make up the time. But the EEO Officer disregarded the Rabbi's letter and she remained silent.

The law requires an employer to reasonably accommodate an employee's religion if it can do so without undue hardship. The law required the EEO Officer either (1) to reasonably accommodate my Sabbath observance or (2) to say undue hardship. But she did neither. Instead she remained silent. I told her that if she did not respond to my request immediately, then I would have to leave on Fridays at 1:00 pm without permission. She replied that she did not condone this type of behavior. Twice I returned to see her but she refused to meet with me. Her silence effectively denied my request. The employer did not do as the law required.

For seven weeks, the EEO Officer remained silent. By her silence, she made me choose between either (1) to obey the requirements of my religion, and to leave work early at 1:00 pm on Fridays, or (2) to obey the requirements of my employment, and to leave work at 4:00 pm on Fridays at the end of the working day. I chose to obey the requirements of my religion and so I left early on Fridays at 1:00 pm but without permission, without agreement and without any accommodation.

I approached the EEO Officer on October 8, 1991. Seven weeks later, on November 27, 1991, the EEO Officer gave her reply. She returned with a counter-offer.

She told me that I had to stay at work until 2:00 pm on Fridays and make up the time. She disregarded the Rabbi's letter and she disregarded the fact that I had left work at 1:00 pm on Fridays the previous year without causing undue hardship. The law requires reasonable accommodation unless undue hardship. I had asked to leave at 1:00 pm and make up the time. She denied my request. She did not say that it would cause undue hardship to grant my request.

Once I did leave at 2:00 pm on a Friday. I found that I had to rush my preparations. Despite rushing, on that evening I arrived late at the Synagogue. The Friday evening Sabbath services had already begun some minutes earlier. Permission to leave at 2:00 pm on Friday and make up the time was not reasonable accommodation because it did not give me the time I needed to travel home from work, prepare for the Sabbath and arrive at the Synagogue on time for Sabbath services.

I approached the EEO Officer on October 8, 1991. Two weeks later, the Department and its managers retaliated against me. On October 23, 1991, the Executive Director revoked my computer password and he brought me up on disciplinary charges. He charged me with personal use of the computer, when, for six months, he had hitherto acquiesced in silence. This action was to be the prelude to a three-year campaign of harassment; a campaign which culminated in my transfer to Rikers Island. I had not anticipated that my request for accommodation for Sabbath observance would trigger such a ferocious response.

CYRIL STEVE NEWMAN - EEO INQUIRY

Action taken:

October 8, 1991	Newman's initial interviewed in reference to his EEO inquiry.
October 9, 1991	Summary of Inquiry submitted to Director of EEO. Conference with Labor Relations re: Sabbath.
October 11, 1991	(Friday) Newman request status and definition of "reasonable". Newman informs investigator that if he did not get a response by the time he should be leaving (1:00pm) he will walk out. This investigator made it clear that the Office of EEO does not condone this type of behavior. Met with Captain Callendar re: Sabbath directive if any.
October 28, 1991	Case conference with Director of EEO.
October 29, 1991	Met with Associate Attorney - Legal Div. in regards to term "reasonable". Called Citywide EEO for guidelines on Religious Accommodations - Spoke with Joel Greenspan.
November 26, 1991	Director of EEO and investigator met with Mr. Steve Newman on accommodation terms. Director of EEO and investigator met with Ray Hickcox, Executive Director of Information Systems.
November 27, 1991	Steve Newman takes medical leave of absence and is expected to return to full duty on February 28, 1992.
December 30, 1991	Timekeeper, Robert Smith was consulted on procedure for change of hours as a result of agreement.
December 31, 1991	Terms and Agreement signed by Ray Hickcox and Patricia M. Mulligan, Director of EEO.

000143

EXHIBIT 1. *EEO Officer's inquiry, dated October 8, 1991 through December 31, 1991.*

DATE: October 9, 1991

TO: Patricia M. Mulligan, Director of EEO

FROM: Rosita Lopez Investigator

SUBJECT: **EEO Inquiry**- Steve Newman

....

Steve Newman, civilian computer Associate who is assigned to Management Information Systems was interviewed October 8, 1991 by this writer.

Mr. Newman has worked for the Department of Correction for 1 1/2 years. His tour is 8amx4pm, Monday to Friday.

He is inquiring if the Agency has defined the term "reasonable" for religious accommodation.

Mr. Newman is questioning if the actions taken by his department head is discriminatory. He has requested permission from his supervisor to leave work every Friday at 1pm (lunch hour 1pm-2pm) to observe the Sabbath.
The previous supervisor had given approval for Mr. Newman to rearrange his weekly schedule so that on Fridays he ended his tour after his lunch hour at 1:00pm and allowed him to make up the 2 hours by working an additional hour each on Mondays and Tuesdays. His present supervisor will not allow him to leave early on Fridays. Mr. Newman is asking if 2 hours a week is considered reasonable accommodation for religious observance.

Approximately 30 days ago Mr. Newman filed a grievance with Labor Relations on this matter, same letter was forwarded to Commissioner Sielaff and Robert Daly.
Mr. Newman has stated that he has not received a reply from anyone.

000158

EXHIBIT 2. *EEO Officer's memorandum about Sabbath observance, dated October 9, 1991.*

K'HAL ADATH JESHURUN קהל עדת ישורון

ב"ה

RAV DR. JOSEPH BREUER זצ"ל
RAV 5700-5740

DR. RAPHAEL MOLLER ז"ל
PRESIDENT 5702-5740

October 23, 1991

To Whom It May Concern:

Mr. Steven Newman is a strictly Orthodox Jew and Sabbath Observer and is a member of our Congregation.

As such, he must leave work on Fridays at 1:00 p.m. in order to be able to be ready for the Sabbath before sundown on Friday. He is willing to make up the time during the rest of the week. Please note that he had a similar arrangement for leaving early last year.

Your cooperation in this matter will be appreciated.

Very truly yours,

K'HAL ADATH JESHURUN

הרב זכרי' געללי
ר"ק
עדת ישורון
נוא יארק, נ.י.
Rav Zachariah Gelley

Rabbi Zachariah Gelley

K'HAL ADATH JESHURUN, INC. • 85-93 Bennett Avenue • New York, N.Y. 10033 • (212) 923-3582 • 923-5936
Fax: 781-4275

EXHIBIT 3. *Rabbi's letter about Sabbath observance, dated October 23, 1991.*

CHAPTER THREE

THE MANAGERS REVOKED MY COMPUTER PASSWORD

WHAT THE JOB INVOLVES: Computer Associates Software under direct supervision, with moderate latitude for independent initiative and judgment, are responsible for the analysis, design, development, implementation, troubleshooting, enhancement, maintenance, and security of database management systems, operating systems, data communication systems, applications, website, and/or related software functions; may supervise staff performing these functions. All Computer Associates Software perform related work.

NEW YORK CITY JOB SPECIFICATION
FOR COMPUTER ASSOCIATE SOFTWARE.

In February 1990, I was appointed to the Information Systems Division of the New York City Department of Correction. I reported for work in April 1990. My official civil service title was Computer Associate Software. I reported directly to the Program Manager.

On my first day of work, the Program Manager issued me with a valid computer password and he assigned me to my desk. The desk had a telephone and a desktop computer. The computer on my desk communicated with the Department's server which, in turn, communicated with the City's IBM mainframe computer system. For the first year, under the direction of the Program Manager, I wrote a series of computer programs used by the Department's Labor Relations unit. In March 1991, the Program Manager assigned me to work on the Visitors Pass system, which I completed in September 1991.

In October 1991, the clocks were set for daylight savings. On October 8, 1991, I approached the EEO Officer to request accommodation for Sabbath observance. On October 23, 1991, two weeks later, the managers abruptly revoked my computer password.

The managers revoked my computer password without any hearing, without any written statement, without any notice, warning, discussion or explanation. Both the telephone and the computer still remained upon my desk, but now I was locked out of the computer. It was no longer possible for me to log into the computer to gain access to the City's computer system. Only two weeks had passed between when I approached the EEO Officer and when the managers revoked my computer password. The reason the managers revoked my password was that I had approached the EEO Officer.

The Department employed me as a Computer Associate Software. The managers revoked my computer password and it was never restored. For over three years, the managers withheld my password. I was a computer programmer but, without a computer password, I could not program the computer. For a computer programmer, having a computer password is not a privilege to be revoked at will - it is a sine qua non of the job.

The managers revoked my password and prevented me from performing the duties for which I had been appointed. The managers intentionally handicapped my work efforts and they set me up for negative performance evaluations and for a transfer to Rikers Island. Neither the Department's Rules nor the Collective Bargaining Agreement had any procedure that provided for grieving the denial of a password. The Union refused to help me. I complained to the EEOC that the Department had revoked my password but the EEOC did not investigate any of my complaints.

In December 1991, I complained to the City Personnel Director that the Department and its managers had revoked my computer password. He wrote to tell the Department that my allegations were serious but there was no reply. In June 1992, I complained to the City Council President that the Department and its managers had revoked my password. He wrote to tell the Department that my allegations were serious. The Commissioner replied but she did not instruct her managers to restore my password.

All of the other computer programmers had valid passwords that enabled them to access the computer. None of the other computer programmers were Jewish. In March 1993, a list of names of authorized users of passwords was issued but my name was not included in the list. In April 1993, the disciplinary charges were adjourned contemplating dismissal, but the Department still did not restore my password or send me on computer training.

In January 1995, the Assistant Commissioner transferred me to Rikers Island. The Telecommunications Director assigned me to sit at a bare desk, with no telephone, with no computer and with no password and nobody to speak with.

One thing leads to another. Because I requested accommodation for Sabbath observance, the managers revoked my computer password. Because they revoked my password, I could not do my job. Because I could not do my job, they called me incompetent and they transferred me to Rikers Island. Because they transferred me to Rikers Island, they increased my commute and they hindered my Sabbath observance.

CHAPTER FOUR

DISCIPLINARY CHARGES

A truth that's told with bad intent
beats all the lies you can invent.
WILLIAM BLAKE.

On April 1, 1991, I made personal use of the computer. There was a computer on my desk. While I worked on the Visitors Pass system, I also made personal use of the computer to type out an essay for class. On October 23, 1991, six months later, the Department charged me that, on April 1, 1991, I did use a Departmental computer for my own personal use without permission or authority from my superior. Such conduct is prejudicial to the good order and discipline of the Department, and in violation of rules and regulations, inefficient performance resulting in work for my own personal purposes as well as of the nature to bring discredit upon the Department.

In September 1991, I completed the Visitors Pass system. This was a highly technical assignment which I completed without help from my supervisor. The Executive Director should have commended me for my work on the Visitors Pass system. Instead, in October 1991, he revoked my computer password and he served disciplinary charges upon me.

On October 23, 1991, the Executive Director revoked my computer password and he served me with disciplinary charges. The charges had three specifications. First, I had raised my voice to my supervisor, second, I had made personal use of the computer and third, I had walked about. On or about the same day as the charges were served on me, my computer password was made invalid. Were the charges true or false? If the charges were true, then I was guilty and I had only myself to blame for the consequences. I should pay the penalty and learn my lesson. If the charges were false, then I could defend myself in a civil service disciplinary hearing, the Judge would find me not guilty and I would suffer no penalty. Not so simple. There is another dimension - were the charges brought in good faith?

The charge that I raised my voice to my supervisor was untrue but the charge that I made personal use of the computer was true and the charge that I walked about was true. Were the disciplinary charges brought in good faith for business reasons? Or was there perhaps some other reason why the managers brought me up on charges?

On March 11, 1991, the Program Manager assigned the Visitors Pass system to me. On March 25, 1991, the Program Manager gave me a satisfactory performance evaluation and I passed my year of probation.

In March 1991, Executive Director Bob Creed became sick and, in April 1991, he left the Department. In March 1991, Raymond Hickox was appointed Executive Director; this is he who had stomped upon the cockroach. He replaced Bob Creed.

In April 1991, Executive Director Hickox called me into his office. He told me that I am obnoxious. He canceled the accommodation for Sabbath observance that Bob Creed had approved. He told me that I had to leave at 4:00 pm on Fridays as he did not approve of employees working irregular hours. He threatened to bring me up on disciplinary charges if I did not complete the Visitors Pass system. I asked to be sent on a CICS training class. "Read the goddamn manual," he replied. But the Executive Director did not warn me not to make personal use of the computer. Why not? Because, at that time, my personal use of the computer was not a matter of concern.

I worked hard, I did as I was told and, on September 20, 1991, I completed the Visitors Pass system. This was a highly technical assignment which I completed on my own. I worked hard to complete the Visitors Pass system and the Executive Director should have commended me for a job well done. Instead he brought me up on charges for misconduct.

The Department charged me with making personal use of the computer. The charge was true. On my desk there was a computer and, on April 1, 1991, I had indeed made personal use of the computer. At the same time as I worked on the Visitors Pass system, I also made personal use of the computer to type out an essay for class. There was no Departmental rule which specifically prohibited personal use of the computer and, at that time my personal use of the computer had not been a matter of concern.

Discipline exercised in good faith requires a prior warning. Before serving me charges, the managers should have warned me against making personal use of the computer. They should have given me an informal warning followed by a written warning followed by a corrective interview. In six months, there had not been any warning at all. Not a peep. For six months, the managers acquiesced in silence and the silence was telling. Sherlock Holmes solved his mystery by the curious incident of the dog that did not bark. It was because I approached the EEO Officer that the managers charged me with personal use of the computer.

The law protects my right to request accommodation for Sabbath observance, but it was my approach to the EEO Officer on October 8, 1991, to request accommodation, that jolted the managers into taking action against me. Two weeks later, they revoked my computer password and charged me with personal use of the computer. They reached back into their memory to look for a complaint that they could bring against me and they recalled that, six months previously, on April 1, 1991, I had made personal use of the computer. Only then did my personal use of the computer become a matter of concern. The managers quickly put pen to paper and they wrote up the charges. Without any warning, they pounced on me with full-blown charges of personal use of the computer.

On October 8, 1991, I approached the EEO Officer to request accommodation for Sabbath observance. On October 23, 1991, the managers brought disciplinary charges against me. The law says that a passage of less than three weeks between my approaching the EEO Officer and the managers serving the disciplinary charges satisfies a prima facie case of retaliation. ("Mickey"). The reason why the managers revoked my computer password and brought the charges is retaliation for my having requested accommodation for Sabbath observance.

The Department and its managers treated me differently and worse than the other computer programmers. None of the managers were Jewish. None of the other computer programmers were Jewish. During the time that I was employed in the Department, no disciplinary charges were served on any of the other computer programmers. I was not the only Jew employed by the Department, and the managers did not say that they hated Jews. But because I approached the EEO

Officer to request accommodation for Sabbath observance, I had transgressed the bounds of their tolerance. I was the wrong sort of Jew!

The Department charged me with walking about. The charge was true. Yes, I did walk about. The managers should have commended me for completing the Visitors Pass system but instead they charged me with walking about. There was no Departmental rule that prohibits walking about. The Assistant Commissioner was always walking up and down the Information Systems office. Furthermore, he walked about while smoking cigarettes and he set fire to the wastepaper basket. But he was never brought up on charges for walking about. Nor was he ever brought up on charges for setting fire to the wastepaper basket. The Department and its managers did not apply discipline even-handedly. They had been more strict with me than they had been with the Assistant Commissioner.

The Department charged me with raising my voice to my supervisor. The charge was untrue. No, I had not raised my voice to my supervisor. A co-worker signed a statement saying that he witnessed me raising my voice to my supervisor. Later, in May 1992, in an affidavit, the co-worker retracted his statement and he swore that he had not seen or heard anything. He swore that he signed his statement because the Program Manager had told him to sign the statement. The Program Manager resigned in August 1992.

I was out sick from November 1991 until March 1992 because I was so upset. The Program Manager was my immediate supervisor and he should have sent me a get-well card. In three months, no one from the Department sent me a get-well card or telephoned me to ask of my welfare, to wish for my recovery and to hope that I would soon come back to work. The managers had no compassion. They showed no care or concern for my health and well-being.

The managers revoked my computer password and served me with charges. This was just the first strike. The managers launched a protracted campaign of harassment and discrimination against me. The campaign lasted for over three years. They harassed me and harassed me. The Deputy Commissioner for Trials and Litigation later told me that the disciplinary process had been used for a purpose for which it was not intended. In April 1993, the disciplinary charges were adjourned, but the managers did not restore my computer password. Because I had no computer password, I could not program the computer.

In January 1995, the managers transferred me to work at Rikers Island. I had endured over three years of harassment and now I resigned. From the day that the managers served charges upon me, they had intended either to terminate my employment or to cause me to resign.

23 Rev. 3-70

CHARGES AND SPECIFICATIONS

No. ....

DEPARTMENT OF CORRECTION
CITY OF NEW YORK

DATE ....

To: **COMMISSIONER of CORRECTION**
(Through Official Channels)

I Hereby Charge Civilian Cyril Newman I.D. #29133 ...... of Information Services
(Shield or Pass No.) (Inst. or Division)

with Violation of Rules and Regulations

SPECIFICATIONS

In that — 1. Said Computer Associate, Cyril Newman on or about August 27, 1991 while speaking to his superior, Patrick Baselice did raise his voice and refuse to let Mr. Baselice out of the office. In doing so, Mr. Newman used his body to block the doorway and refused to let Mr. Baselice pass. Mr. Baselice asked Mr. Newman to let him through and Mr. Newman refused. Mr. Baselice was forced to pick up Mr. Newman's arm and move him aside. Mr. Newman's conduct is insubordinate, and disrespectful to a superior, constituted disobeyal of an order, and a failure to maintain a gentlemanly demeanor. It was also prejudicial to the good order and discipline of the department, and of a nature to bring discredit upon the Department.

Rules: 3.15.010
3.15.030
3.15.140
3.15.150
3.15.250

2. Said Computer Associate Cyril Newman on or about April 1, 1991 and on or about September 20, 1991 did use a departmental computer for his own personal use without permission or authority from his superior. Such conduct is prejudicial to the good order and discipline of the department, and in violation of rules and regulations, inefficient performance resulting in work for his personal purposes as well as of the nature to bring discredit upon the Department.

Rules: 3.05.080
3.15.020
3.15.070
3.15.250

3. Said Computer Associate, Cyril Newman, on or about July 31, 1991 was given a direct order by a superior to stop walking around the corridors and hallways of his work unit, and to return to his desk and continue his work. Mr. Newman proceeded to reply that he was working, and failed to obey his superior's orders to return to his desk. Such conduct is

EXHIBIT 4. *Disciplinary charges, served October 23, 1991.*

23 Rev. 3-70

CHARGES AND SPECIFICATIONS

No. ....

DEPARTMENT OF CORRECTION
CITY OF NEW YORK

DATE ....

To: **COMMISSIONER of CORRECTION**
(Through Official Channels)

I Hereby Charge Civilian Cyril Newman I.D. #29133 (*Shield or Pass No.*) of Information Services (*Inst. or Division*)

with Violation of Rules and Regulations

SPECIFICATIONS

In that — 1. insubordination, inefficient performance, and a violation of Departmental rules and regulations in that Mr. Newman left his work site without permission of his superior. His actions were also prejudicial to the good order and discipline of the Department.

Rules: 3.05.080
3.05.090
3.15.030
3.15.090
3.15.250

p.242.

Allison lewis-Smith
Deputy Commissioner
Trials and Litigation

EXHIBIT 4. *Continued.*

THE CITY OF NEW YORK
DEPARTMENT OF CORRECTION
60 HUDSON STREET
NEW YORK, N.Y. 10013-4393

ALLYN R. SIELAFF
COMMISSIONER

EDWARD J. ALLOCCO
DEPUTY COMMISSIONER
OF ADMINISTRATION

TO: Steven Newman, Computer Associate

FROM: Raymond Hickcox, Executive Director, IS

DATE: November 21, 1991

SUBJECT: ADMINS TRAINING COURSE

Your request to be provided training in ADMINS has been denied, as the course is available only to employees working in IIS. In the event courses for which you are eligible become available, your request for training will be considered.

cc: Douglas Waldman, Director, IIS

EXHIBIT 5. *Denial of Admins training, dated November 21, 1991.*

CHAPTER FIVE

STEP ONE CONFERENCE

We're off to see the Wizard, the wonderful Wizard of Oz.
YIP HARBURG.

On November 27, 1991, under the Union-City Collective Bargaining Agreement, the Executive Director held a Step One Conference. The purpose of this Conference was to present to the Union the charges which he had served upon me on October 23, 1991. Three people were present at this Conference; the Executive Director, the Union Representative and myself. The Executive Director recommended suspension without pay from my employment for forty-five days, fifteen days for each charge. The Union Representative said forty-five days is too long for a first offense and it violates the principle of progressive discipline. There was little discussion. No one raised their voice or banged the table. This was a formalistic ritual presentation of charges. The meeting lasted for only a few minutes.

After the meeting was over, the Representative recommended to me that I plead guilty to one of the charges in exchange for the other two charges being dropped, and serve only fifteen days out of the recommended forty-five days of suspension. She had not given me sound advice. She had already judged my case and decided against me. She was too eager to plead me guilty. She gave me no hope. With friends like the Union, who needs enemies?

I had not become a civil servant to spend my career defending myself from disciplinary charges. I had completed the Visitors Pass system and the managers should have commended me for my accomplishments, not served me with charges. On April 1, 1991, I made personal use of the computer, and the managers acquiesced in silence. On October 8, 1991, I approached the EEO Officer. Two weeks later, on October 23, 1991, the managers revoked my computer password and they brought me up on charges. None of the other computer programmers had been served charges and they all had their passwords.

On Wednesday, November 27, 1991, the same day as the Step One Conference took place, the EEO Officer returned to me. She told me that I could leave at 2:00 pm on Friday and make up the time. She told me that I could not leave work at 1:00 pm on Fridays and make up the time. I was upset with the disciplinary charges preferred against me at the Step One Conference. I was so upset that the next day, November 28, 1991, I went out on sick leave. I did not return to work until March 2, 1992.

CHAPTER SIX

MEETING WITH UNION PSYCHIATRIST

I'm not really bad, I'm just misunderstood.
Deep down inside me there is good.
STEPHEN SONDHEIM.

I was out sick for three months, from November 28, 1991 until March 2, 1992. The Union secured the approval of Correction's Personnel Division for me to take sick leave. While I was out sick, I met with the Union's social worker and the Union paid me a stipend for my temporary disability. This stipend was thereabouts a third of the wage which I usually earned at the Department of Correction. From December 1991 until January 1992, I met once a week with the Union's social worker.

I completed the Visitors Pass system. I approached the EEO Officer. The managers revoked my computer password and served me with disciplinary charges. I asked the social worker to refer me to see a Union lawyer to discuss my legal rights but she did not make the referral.

The meetings with the Union's social worker were unproductive and they left me confused and demoralized. She wrote that I was *"anxious, belligerent, angry, defended [sic], agitated, paranoid, grandiose...very blaming and projecting onto others all of his problems, fantasizing that all is boss's fault."* I was not "projecting" onto my managers. I was angry because I had completed the Visitors Pass system and I did not deserve to be served charges. This was not a "paranoid fantasy." The charges were very real. Why was the social worker so obtuse that she could not see that the managers had caused the problems by serving me with charges?

After several weeks, the social worker referred me to see a Union psychiatrist. The meeting took place in January 1992. Both the social worker and my wife came with me to this meeting. The psychiatrist did not greet me or begin with small talk to put me at ease. He got straight to the point.

"The reason you are having problems is that your managers are not satisfied with your work performance," he said.

"How can that be? I have documentation which will show that I single-handedly completed a highly technical computer assignment."

"All the documentation will show is that the managers were not satisfied with your work performance."

"You are a quack!"

I left the meeting with the psychiatrist and I never returned to see him or the social worker. Another Union psychiatrist then diagnosed me as "borderline schizophrenic." He had never even met with me. The Union had more quacks than a duck pond.

The managers revoked my computer password, they served me with charges and they intended to terminate my employment. The Union did nothing to help. I was a permanent tenured civil servant and I had completed the Visitors Pass system. I took charge of the situation and charted my own course. In March 1992, I returned to work.

CHAPTER SEVEN

SEEKING OUTSIDE HELP

In March 1991, I complained to the Union about the out of title Visitors Pass system but the Union Representative told me that the work was not out of title and she refused to file my grievance. She told me that the management have a right to mismanage. I filed my own out of title grievance, pursuant to the Department's Rules and Regulations.

In October 1991, I requested accommodation for Sabbath observance. The Executive Director revoked my computer password and he served me with disciplinary charges. The charges had three specifications. First, I had raised my voice to my supervisor, second, I had made personal use of the computer and third, I had walked about. The Representative promised to grieve the charges according to the Union-City grievance procedure. As to the managers revoking my password, she told me that the management have a right to mismanage.

In November 1991, I met with the Inspector General about two matters. First, concerning the Executive Director. I complained to the Inspector General that the Executive Director had revoked my computer password and served me with charges because I requested accommodation for Sabbath observance. The Inspector General took no action. Second, concerning the Program Manager. I told the Inspector General that the Program Manager was living at an address outside of the City, contrary to the City's rules that require City employees to reside within the City. The Inspector General took no action.

In December 1991, I complained to the U.S. Equal Employment Opportunity Commission that the Department and its managers revoked my computer password and they served disciplinary charges upon me because I requested accommodation for Sabbath observance. I complained that the Department did not give me the training that had been given to the other computer programmers. An officer of the EEOC took my notarized statement and she opened a file.

Subsequently I amended my complaint to the EEOC by bringing additional complaints. I complained that the Department did not give me the training that had been given to the other computer programmers. Each year, the other computer programmers were given two or three weeks of training in computer development tools such as Admins. I was given no training at all. I complained the managers harassed me and that my supervisor shouted at me and that he attempted to demote me. I complained to the EEOC that the managers gave me inappropriate work assignments and negative performance evaluations because I requested accommodation for Sabbath observance. The EEOC took my statements and updated my complaint. But the EEOC did not investigate any of my complaints or protect me from the harassment. The Union did not accompany me on any of my visits to the EEOC.

Also in December 1991, I complained to the City Personnel Director that the managers revoked my computer password and served me with disciplinary charges. He wrote to the Commissioner for Correction saying that I had made serious allegations. There was no reply from the Department. In January 1992, I met with the Department of Correction's Deputy Commissioner for Trials and Litigation concerning the disciplinary charges.

In February 1992, I wrote to the Commissioner for Investigation concerning my supervisor, the Program Manager. I reported to the Commissioner for Investigation that, according to the telephone directory White Pages, his driving license and his voting record, these are all public records, the Program Manager was living at an address outside of the City and this was contrary to the City's rules that require City employees to reside within the City. Also in February 1992, I met with my City Council Member who contacted the Commissioner for Investigation.

In June 1992, I complained to the City Council President that the managers revoked my computer password and served me with disciplinary charges. He warned the Commissioner for Correction that I had made serious allegations.

CHAPTER EIGHT

MEETING WITH DEPUTY COMMISSIONER FOR TRIALS

I started work in April 1990. In October 1991, the Executive Director served me with disciplinary charges. In November 1991, he held a Step One Conference to present those charges to the Union. The Department recommended suspension without pay from my employment for forty-five days, fifteen days for each of the three charges. I had worked hard to complete the Visitors Pass system and the Department and its managers should have commended me. Instead they served disciplinary charges upon me. From November 1991 until March 1992, I was out sick because I was so upset.

In January 1992, my wife requested a meeting with the Correction Department's Deputy Commissioner for Trials and Litigation. The Deputy Commissioner agreed to meet with us. This was a private unofficial meeting. Neither the Union Representative nor the Executive Director were informed or invited to attend.

The Deputy Commissioner was the person who had authorized and who had signed the disciplinary charges. She told us that she did not agree with the charges, that there had been an abuse of process and that the disciplinary process had been used for a purpose for which it was not intended. She told us that she had signed the charges under protest because she had been ordered to do so. She could not void the charges but she could help me. She recommended that I defend myself before the Office of Administrative Trials and Hearings (OATH), rather than through the Union grievance procedure. She promised to appoint a prosecutor whom I would find sympathetic.

It had been a relief to speak with to the Deputy Commissioner. At long last, someone in authority, someone who knew what was going on, had told me that the charges were unfair. I could hardly believe my ears. She gave me hope and encouragement. She was the one who had authorized the charges against me, she was my adversary but yet she was resolutely on my side and she wanted me to beat the charges. She helped me and the managers never again brought charges against me. With adversaries like the Deputy Commissioner, who needs friends? The next week, the Deputy Commissioner resigned from the Department.

CHAPTER NINE

MEETING WITH MY CITY COUNCIL MEMBER

In February 1992, I met with the City Council Member who represented northern Manhattan. The Council Member would not arrange to void the charges. Instead he offered to arrange a transfer for me to work in another City agency. He said that it would be a second chance and I could start afresh with new managers.

A second chance implies that I had failed the first time around. But I had not failed. I had completed the Visitors Pass system and I deserved a commendation. It would not be a fresh start for me to transfer to a new City agency while the charges from the old City agency were still hanging over me. A fresh start would have to include voiding the disciplinary charges prior to transferring to a new City agency.

Moreover a new City agency might require me to serve another year of probation. I had already served one year of probation to earn my permanent Civil Service appointment. I should not have to earn my permanent appointment a second time. I should not have to serve a second year of probation in a new agency, while my supervisors had never served a single day of probation. I would only have been willing to transfer to a new City agency on condition that (1) the charges were voided and that (2) I did not have to serve probation. The Council Member was not making this offer. For the time being, the best chance of surviving in my employment with the City would be for me to remain a permanent tenured civil servant in my current employment at the Department of Correction.

I waited for the EEOC to investigate my complaints. I had already reported to the Commissioner for Investigation that the Program Manager had violated the City's rule concerning residency. Meanwhile the Council Member wrote to the Commissioner for Investigation to remind the Department to investigate whether the Program Manager had violated the City's residency requirement.

PART TWO

DISCIPLINARY CHARGES ARE ADJOURNED CONTEMPLATING DISMISSAL

CHAPTER TEN

SUMMARY OF SITUATION SO FAR

The Jewish religion mandates the observance of the Sabbath. In winter 1990-1991, the previous year, the Department accommodated my Sabbath observance. I left on Fridays at 1:00 pm for Sabbath observance and made up the time. This is an arrangement that I had worked out with the first Executive Director and with the Program Manager. No other employee's working hours needed to be changed for this accommodation. No one asserted that this accommodation had caused the Department undue hardship.

In March 1991, Executive Director Bob Creed became sick and, in April 1991, he left the Department. In March 1991, Raymond Hickox was appointed Executive Director. He replaced Bob Creed.

In April 1991, Executive Director Hickox called me into his office. He told me that I am obnoxious. He canceled the accommodation for Sabbath observance that Bob Creed had approved. He told me that I had to leave at 4:00 pm on Fridays as he did not approve of employees working irregular hours. He threatened to bring me up on disciplinary charges if I did not complete the Visitors Pass system.

In October 1991, the clocks were set for daylight savings. This year, the winter of 1991-1992, my need to observe the Sabbath was to become a problem. I spoke to my supervisor, the Program Manager. He told me that he did not object to my leaving early on Friday. However, he told me that Systems Director, did object to my leaving early. On October 4, 1991, I approached the new Executive Director to request accommodation to observe the Sabbath. He remained silent and he did not grant my request. Then on October 8, 1991, I approached the Department of Correction's Equal Employment Opportunity officer. I told her that I needed an accommodation to leave work at 1:00 pm on Fridays for Sabbath observance and to make up the time. I told her this is the arrangement that I had in 1990. I told her that I had approached the current Executive Director but he remained silent. I submitted a letter from the Rabbi of my Synagogue but the EEO Officer disregarded the letter. She remained silent and she did not grant my request.

I approached the EEO Officer on October 8, 1991, but she did not respond until November 27, 1991. For each of those seven Friday afternoons that had passed by, the Department and its managers had not in any way accommodated my Sabbath observance, not by a single minute. There had been no accommodation whatsoever. On October 23, 1991, two weeks after I approached the EEO Officer, the Executive Director revoked my computer password. Also he served disciplinary charges upon me.

On November 27, 1991, two events took place. First, the Executive Director held the Step One Conference and he presented the disciplinary charges to the Union. These charges alleged that I raised my voice to my supervisor, that I made personal use of the computer and that I walked about. Then second, the EEO Officer came to me. She told me that the Department had denied my request to leave at 1:00 pm on Fridays and make up the time. Instead she had a counter-offer. She said that I had to stay at work until 2:00 pm on Fridays and make up the time.

This was one hour later than I had requested and I was not going to haggle. Permission to leave at 2:00 pm on Friday and make up the time was not reasonable accommodation because it did not give me the time I needed to travel home from work, prepare for the Sabbath and arrive at the Synagogue on time for Sabbath services.

Federal law requires an employer to reasonably accommodate an employee's religion if it can do so without undue hardship. The previous year, in winter 1990-1991, I had left at 1:00 pm on Friday, and made up the time, and this had not caused any undue hardship to the Department. This year, October and November 1991, I continued to leave at 1:00 pm on Fridays. On October 8, 1991, I approached the EEO Officer but she did not approve my request to leave at 1:00 pm on Fridays. My leaving early at 1:00 pm on Fridays was unauthorized. I left early on Fridays without permission, without agreement and without any accommodation. The EEO Officer told me that she did not condone this type of behavior, but she did not say that this would cause undue hardship to the Department.

The refusal by the managers to let me leave at 1:00 pm on Friday this year was unreasonable. They refused to let me leave at 1:00 pm on Fridays, and make up the time, not because it would cause undue hardship, but because they resented my Sabbath observance. They served me with charges because I requested accommodation for Sabbath observance. No matter what obstacles the managers placed in my way, I was determined to observe the Sabbath.

I approached the EEO Officer. Two weeks later, the managers served disciplinary charges. By scheduling the Step One Conference and the EEO Officer's reply to occur both on the same day, the Department and its managers reinforced the link between my Sabbath observance and the disciplinary charges and thereby they delivered to me a clear and emphatic message: we do not want Jews to observe the Sabbath, and your request is denied. Moreover, because you approached the EEO Officer to make this request, we shall terminate your employment. I was so upset that the next day I went out sick and I did not return to work until March 1992.

In the winter of 1990-1991 there had been no problem and the original Executive Director had accommodated my Sabbath observance. I left work early on Fridays at 1:00 pm and made up the time. In March 1991, I received a satisfactory performance evaluation. In April 1991, a new Executive Director had been appointed. He told me that he did not approve of employees working irregular hours. From then on, the Department and its managers did not reasonably accommodate my Sabbath observance. In October 1991, the clocks were set for daylight savings. On October 8, 1991, I approached the EEO Officer to request accommodation for Sabbath observance. On October 23, 1991, the managers revoked my computer password and served me with disciplinary charges.

In November 1991, I met the Inspector General of the Department of Correction. I complained that the managers revoked my computer password and served me with disciplinary charges because I approached the EEO officer but he took no action. In December 1991, I complained to the City Personnel Director. He wrote to the Commissioner for Correction saying that I had made serious allegations. The Commissioner and the Department did not reply.

In December 1991, I complained to the EEOC that the Department and its managers revoked my computer password and brought me up on charges because I requested accommodation for Sabbath observance. I waited for the EEOC to investigate my complaint.

CHAPTER ELEVEN

MEETING WITH DEPARTMENT'S EEO DIRECTOR

It doesn't matter what you believe
just so long as you're sincere.
CHARLES M. SCHULZ.

In March 1992, I returned to work from sick leave. Upon my return to work, the Department's EEO Director directed me to appear before her. She wrote, *"You are directed to appear in this office...Your failure to appear will be considered a failure on your part to cooperate in good faith efforts to resolve the matter you complained of."*

My failure? My good faith? The managers had not shown any good faith, goodwill, trust, honest dealing or respect. They had revoked my password and served me with charges. I did not appreciate the EEO Director questioning my good faith. She had a law degree but she was unsympathetic and she mishandled my complaint. Directed to appear? She summonsed me to appear before her office as if she had been the magistrate and I had been the accused.

I asked the Union Representative to accompany me to my meeting with the EEO Director. Instead of agreeing to accompany me to the meeting, the Union Representative replied to me with an expletive. I had to go on my own to meet with the EEO Director.

My first winter, October 1990, I had left at 1:00 pm on Fridays for Sabbath observance and made up the times;

and there had been no undue hardship to the Department. In October 1991, I requested an accommodation to leave at 1:00 pm on Fridays for Sabbath observance, and make up the time and I submitted a letter from my Rabbi.

The Sabbath arrives every Friday evening. Seven Fridays had passed since I had made my request, from October 8, 1991 until November 27, 1991, but the Department had done nothing to accommodate my Sabbath observance. The EEO Director explained that the Department has a formal procedure for handling EEO complaints. According to this procedure, the Department has two months to respond to a request or to a complaint. In this case, she said, the Department had indeed responded within two months.

Federal law requires an employer to reasonably accommodate an employee's religious observance and practice if it can do so without undue hardship. It brooks no two-month delay. At no time did the EEO Officer, EEO Director or any manager, say that it would cause undue hardship to the Department if I were to leave at 1:00 pm on Friday and make up the time.

The EEO Director disregarded the Rabbi's letter. She told me that I could not leave until 2:00 pm on Fridays. This was an hour later than I had requested. She did not say that 1:00 pm on Fridays would cause undue hardship to the Department. In winter 1990, I had left at 1:00 pm on Fridays, and made up the time; and this accommodation had not caused undue hardship to the Department. For the EEO Director to refuse to repeat the same accommodation in winter 1991 was not reasonable. She told me that she had offered to let me leave at 2:00 pm on Fridays and make up the time. She told me that she would record that she had offered me a reasonable accommodation and that I had rejected her offer.

I complained to the EEO Director that the Department and its managers had revoked my computer password and brought me up on charges to retaliate because I had requested accommodation for Sabbath observance. I was out sick for three months. The EEO Director refused to investigate my complaint. She told me that the Department had a formal complaint procedure which required the complaint to be put into writing. She said that because I had not put my complaint in writing, therefore I had not properly followed the Department's formal complaint procedure, therefore I had not made any complaint, therefore there was no retaliation for my having made a complaint.

In writing? Where did she get that from? I approached the EEO Officer to request accommodation for Sabbath observance. Two weeks later, the Department revoked my computer password and served charges against me. The Constitution guarantees freedom of speech, freedom of religion and the right to petition the government for redress of grievance. Federal law requires employers to accommodate religious observance and it prohibits employers from retaliating against employees for requesting accommodation. The law does not say that the request by an employee for accommodation for Sabbath observance must be put in writing. The EEO Director was making up her own rules as she went along.

These were the three matters of dispute. (1) The EEO Director would not let me leave until 2:00 pm on Fridays and make up the time. But I was requesting to leave at 1:00 pm on Fridays and make up the time. (2) She demanded that I acknowledged the Department's reasonable accommodation. But from October 8, 1991 until November 27, 1991, the Department had not accommodated my Sabbath observance at all. (3) She demanded that I acknowledged that she had made a sincere attempt to mediate my complaint. But she refused to investigate my complaint that the managers had retaliated against me because I requested accommodation for Sabbath observance.

The EEO Director presented me with an agreement that she had written and prepared for me to sign. I asked to take a copy of the proposed agreement home to think about it but she would not give me a copy to take outside the room. She was impatient with me and she demanded that I signed this document there and then. She demanded that I acknowledged the Department's reasonable accommodation and that she had made a sincere attempt to mediate my complaint. I had no input, I did not agree with the terms, the document was a diktat, she refused to change a single word; and so I refused to sign her agreement.

The EEO Director had questioned my good faith and I was not convinced of her sincerity. The managers sincerely intended to terminate my employment. I sincerely pursued my complaint of employment discrimination against the managers. The meeting was a train wreck. I continued to leave early at 1:00 pm on Fridays to observe the Sabbath; but I did so without permission, without agreement and without any accommodation.

In the winter months, the Sabbath arrives early in the afternoon but, in winter 1991, the managers did not accommodate my Sabbath observance. I had completed the Visitors Pass system and the managers intended to terminate my employment. Nothing that I did, or did not do, would make any difference. So I might just as well leave early at 1:00 pm on Fridays during the summer, as well as during the winter, because this way I had extra time to prepare for the Sabbath. The managers never raised any objection to my leaving early on Fridays in summer.

CHAPTER ELEVEN

After I complained to the EEO Director, the managers continued their three-year campaign of harassment and discrimination against me. They gave me negative performance evaluations and a corrective interview. They transferred me to Rikers Island and they subjected me to intolerable working conditions.

CHAPTER TWELVE

COMMISSIONER FOR CORRECTION REPLIES TO THE CITY COUNCIL PRESIDENT

A prince should appear merciful, faithful, humane, upright, and religious.
MACHIAVELLI.

In May 1992, Mayor David Dinkins appointed a new Commissioner for Correction. Her name was Catherine Abate. She had a law degree. From 1986 until 1992, she had been the Executive Deputy Commissioner of the New York State Division of Human Rights.

Catherine Abate's father had been a captain in the Mafia. At first she denied this and she said that the allegation was bias against Italian-Americans. Later she admitted that the allegation might be true. Upon taking office she published a statement saying that she expected vigorous efforts to create a workplace environment where everybody is treated with dignity.

In June 1992, the City Council President warned her that my allegations were serious. The Commissioner straightaway replied that the Department's EEO office had completed an internal investigation, that my Sabbath was being accommodated, that my out of title grievance was without merit and that I was facing disciplinary charges. She wrote that the Department takes all complaints of employment discrimination very seriously and that it is "making every effort to resolve the issues."

Dignity? Resolve the issues? The Commissioner talked about everybody being treated with dignity, and she sounded as benevolent as Good King Wenceslas, but she did nothing. The Commissioner did not meet with me and her reply did not address my complaints. She did not explain why the Department had revoked my computer password and she did not order her managers to restore my computer password. She did not void the disciplinary charges or order the EEO Director to investigate whether the charges had been brought against me because I requested accommodation for Sabbath observance.

The Commissioner told the City Council President that the Department was accommodating my Sabbath observance. But her Department and her managers revoked my computer password and served me with disciplinary charges because I had requested accommodation for Sabbath observance. Then they transferred me to work at Rikers Island. The transfer made my commute home longer and this complicated my Sabbath observance.

The managers intended to terminate my employment. The harassment and discrimination continued unabated. The Commissioner had been warned that I had made serious allegations. She was indifferent to my complaints. She knew and approved of action taken against me. She made no effort to resolve the issues and she took no corrective action.

The Department of Correction newsletter published a photograph of the Commissioner meeting with some schoolchildren in her office. It was nice of the Commissioner to find the time to meet with the children. But she never once stepped foot in the Information Systems Division to meet with the staff. Nor did she ever find the time to meet with me to hear my complaints. She did not instruct her managers to restore my computer password and she did not take my complaints very seriously.

THE CITY OF NEW YORK
DEPARTMENT OF CORRECTION
60 HUDSON STREET
NEW YORK, N.Y. 10013-4393

OCMA-92/555

CATHERINE M. ABATE
COMMISSIONER

June 30, 1992

Mr. Seth Diamond
Special Counsel
The City of New York
The President of the City Council
City Hall
New York, N.Y. 10007

Dear Mr. Diamond:

The Department of Correction is in receipt of your letter regarding the employment discrimination complaint of Mr. Cyril Stephen Newman.

The Department's Equal Employment Opportunity Office has completed an internal investigation into a complaint of employment discrimination previously filed by Mr. Newman, the result of which was to accommodate Mr. Newman with respect to his working hours and his observance of the Sabbath. Mr. Newman subsequently filed with both the New York State Division of Human Rights and the Equal Employment Opportunity Commission external complaints which are currently under investigation. Further, please be advised that an out of title grievance was also filed by Mr. Newman and has been heard at a Step 3 hearing through the grievance procedure of the Mayor's Office of Labor Relations and was found to be without merit. In addition, the disciplinary charges referred to in Mr. Newman's letter are being handled by our agency's Trial Division.

The Department of Correction takes very seriously all complaints of employment discrimination and is making every effort to resolve the issues presented in this case.

If I can be of further assistance please contact me at (212) 266-1212.

Sincerely,

Catherine M. Abate

Catherine M. Abate
Commissioner

EXHIBIT 6. *Commissioner's reply to City Council President, dated June 30, 1992.*

CHAPTER THIRTEEN

INAPPROPRIATE AND DEGRADING MAKE-WORK DUTIES

Yo heave ho! Once more, once again, still once more!
VOLGA BOATMEN.

In February 1990, the New York City Department of Correction appointed me from the civil service list for Computer Associate Software to the Information Systems Division. I reported for work in April 1990. The Department provided me with a valid computer password to access the computer. I was a computer programmer and I reported directly to the Program Manager. For the first year, I wrote a series of computer programs used by the Department's Labor Relations unit. By April 1991, I had served a year of probation and the Program Manager gave me a satisfactory performance evaluation. I was now a permanent tenured civil servant.

In October 1991, I requested accommodation for Sabbath observance. Two weeks later the managers revoked my password and brought me up on charges. The managers intended to terminate my employment or force me to resign. The Department employed me as a computer programmer but, without having a computer password, I could not program the computer. The managers interfered with my work performance, handicapped my work efforts and set me up for negative performance evaluations and a corrective interview.

The New York City Job Specification for Computer Associate Software specifies the duties for which I had been appointed. These duties involve analysis, design, development, implementation, troubleshooting, enhancement, maintenance, and security of database management systems, operating systems, data communication systems, applications, website, and/or related software functions. But I could not do any of this because the managers had revoked my computer password and prevented me from performing the duties for which I had been appointed.

All of the other computer programmers worked together as a team on the Inmate Information system. They all had valid passwords that enabled them to access the computer. None of the other computer programmers were Jewish. The Executive Director instructed me to write a manual on project life cycles. I was a computer programmer and I knew nothing at all about project life cycles. None of the other computer programmers were instructed to write a manual on project life cycles.

Between March 1991 and September 1991, with little supervision, I completed the highly technical Visitors Pass system. Surely this proves that I was competent. Came the day when the managers revoked my password. For a computer programmer, a computer password is a critical tool of the job. By revoking my password, the managers prevented me from doing my job. Because I could not do my job, they called me incompetent. The more often they repeated to each other that I did no work, the more indignant they waxed. It is a well-documented entomological phenomenon that grasshoppers will not hop when their legs are removed. Well, duh! What did the managers expect?

In June 1992, Executive Director Hickox told me that, from now on, I was to report to the Director for

Systems Development. The Systems Director's name was Mr. Douglas E. Waldmann. He sat in an office which was only a few feet away from my cubicle. Was there a personality conflict between me and the Systems Director? For the first two years after I joined the Department, he and I had never spoken to each other. I was barely aware that he even existed.

Systems Director Waldmann sat in his office reading the newspaper except when he attended management meetings. He did not venture forth. He did not receive visitors and he did not speak on the phone. Every day, the door of his office was open, and he just sat there reading the newspaper. He had been appointed from the civil service list for Staff Analyst. Later on, the Department promoted him to the rank of Deputy Commissioner. He had a Master's degree in Psychology and he was a Vietnam veteran. However he had neither passed a civil service computer exam, nor had he ever written a computer program.

My first meeting with Systems Director Waldmann got off to a surprisingly good start. He gave me a rice cake and I told him that I looked forward to working with him. Meanwhile he did not restore my computer password and the disciplinary charges were still hanging over me. He failed to provide appropriate and supportive supervision.

In January 1993, the Executive Director gave me a memorandum which ordered me not to read the newspaper during working hours. He wrote that it was inappropriate. Meanwhile the Systems Director sat in his office reading the newspaper but the Department took no action against him. He gave me a memorandum which prohibited me from speaking to co-workers. He did not say good morning or please or thank you. Once he shouted at me. We rarely met.

Whenever we met, the Systems Director addressed me in an arrogant and disrespectful tone. Instead of saying, "please do this," he would say, "you have been given a direct order to do this. Are you refusing to obey a direct order?" He gave me so many direct orders that my head was spinning. The Department Rules say that a subordinate must salute his superior so, whenever I saw him, I saluted him. Then he attempted to have me served charges because I saluted him. I kept a diary on the managers and the Systems Director kept a diary on me. His diary was provided to me by Corporation Counsel during discovery. Here is an example of what he wrote:

"6/8 9:52 Disobeyed direct order to come into my office. I went to get a cup of water in men's room. When I returned he was standing in front of reception desk saluting me. I said "I want to see you in my office." He said "Do I hear a please." I said "No, I want to see you in my office." He then went to his cubicle. I got Thierry and in the presence of Steward and Maureen, he refused my direct order to go into my office. He said "are you going to say please." I said no. He still refused."

When I worked on the Visitors Pass system, I requested training in CICS, but the Executive Director told me to learn CICS by studying a CICS manual. All of the other computer programmers worked as a team on the Inmate Information System. Every year, the other computer programmers were given two or three weeks of computer training. They received training in Admins, a proprietary computer development tool. I requested training in Admins but the Executive Director denied my application. While the other computer programmers were sent on training classes to learn Admins, I was left behind. The Assistant Commissioner ordered me to work on an IIS project and to study the Admins manual.

In June 1993, the Systems Director shouted at me that I was incompetent and crazy. I complained to the Assistant Commissioner but he took no action against the Systems Director. Instead the Assistant Commissioner wrote to tell the Commissioner that I was incompetent and that I did absolutely no work. The managers intended to terminate my employment, they revoked my computer password and they did not send me on training courses with the other computer programmers.

The Systems Director instructed me to document old obsolete computer programs. This was not my job. This was sham make-work. He gave me make-work duties which disguised that I was no longer doing computer programming work. It is inconceivable that there was any business purpose to this documentation. It was work for work's sake. He gave me this sham make-work to undermine my morale, to discourage me from pursuing my complaint of discrimination, to discriminate against me and to cause me to resign.

Documenting the old obsolete computer programs was inappropriate and degrading work. He ordered me to repeat the same make-work again and again. The futility of being required to make several efforts to document obsolete computer programs reminded me of the film "Cool Hand Luke" where the prisoner has to dig a hole, fill it, dig the hole and fill it again. The law prohibits retaliatory work assignments that could well dissuade a reasonable worker from making or supporting a charge of discrimination. ("White").

The Systems Director placed me on the horns of a dilemma. Either I redo the work - this proves that I had been unable to complete my assignment, and so I am incompetent and I deserve to lose my job. Or I refuse to redo the work - this proves that I am refusing to obey a direct order, and so I am insubordinate and

I deserve to lose my job. Damned if I do and damned if I don't. He had revoked my computer password and placed me on some kind of modified duty, but without a hearing, without any written statement, without any notice, warning, discussion or explanation.

The Systems Director wrote a slew of hostile memoranda at me. He wrote that my work was unsatisfactory and he threatened me with disciplinary charges to terminate my employment. I had provided complete and accurate documentation of the obsolete computer programs the first time around. I had completed the documentation to the best of my ability. Nevertheless I obeyed the Systems Director's direct orders and I redid the work again and again and again. Every week, and sometimes more than once in a week, he would write a memorandum telling me that my work was unsatisfactory. He gave me direct orders to correct my work and he threatened me with disciplinary action if I failed to obey his direct orders.

In July 1993, the Systems Director gave me a negative performance evaluation which said that my documentation was incomplete and inaccurate and that I had to be told to redo the work several times. The evaluation recommended immediate termination of my employment. Then he wrote to the Assistant Commissioner to recommend immediate termination of my employment. The next week, the Assistant Commissioner transferred me to Personnel Division, in another building. The Systems Director and I never met again but he continued to write to me.

The Systems Director wrote to tell me that the negative performance evaluation proved that I was incompetent. Initially I had tried to redo the work but I found nothing to correct. I stopped redoing the work and I just wrote back that the work which I had done was correct and that it was the best that I could do.

Here is a typical example. In August 1993, one month after he recommended terminating my employment, the Systems Director wrote: *"It is my professional opinion that the documentation you provided is too brief and must be expanded. It is their brevity which renders them inaccurate; expansion of the narrative will correct the problem. As your supervisor, I am directing you to expand this documentation and to produce flow charts. Any failure to expand the documentation and to produce the flow charts will be held as a violation of a direct order."*

My documentation of the programs had been accurate. It was plain and brief. But brevity was not acceptable to the Systems Director. He demanded the documentation to be expansive and verbose. He threatened disciplinary action on account of my writing style. The managers had already brought charges against me so this was no idle threat. This kind of supervision was oppressive and it did not help me with my work. None of the other computer programmers were assigned to documenting the obsolete programs.

Each of us had his job to do. If it were the job of the Systems Director to terminate my employment, then it was my job to resist the termination of my employment. His job was to wear me down by attrition. My job was not to be worn down. If it were the job of the Systems Director to write unhelpful and unedifying memoranda to me, then it was my job to write unhelpful and unedifying memoranda back to the Systems Director. Each of us, the Systems Director and I, worked indefatigably at his job and nothing of value was produced. This is how hard-earned taxpayer dollars were spent. The buck stopped with the Commissioner. The City Council President warned her that I had made serious complaints but she took no corrective action. She did not order her managers to restore my password. The harassment and discrimination continued unabated.

In December 1993, the managers sent me on a two-day course to learn Microsoft DOS. Throughout my more than four years of employment with the Department, this was the only training I received. During these same four years, the other computer programmers had received eight or more weeks of training.

In January 1994, the Systems Director ordered me to apply for a training course to learn Paradox, a computer development tool. Several weeks before the classes were due to start, I submitted my application to attend but he returned it as incomplete and I resubmitted it. He wrote back, *"Today I received the application, which was again incomplete and sloppily filled out... Your continued refusal to provide the Department with the necessary information on the training form raises serious questions about your interest in training and your commitment to your job."* Each time I resubmitted the application form for the Paradox course, he was not satisfied. Only once the classes were over, and it was too late for me to attend, did he finally approve my application. I was the only computer programmer in the Department who did not attend the Paradox course.

In December 1991, I complained to the EEOC. While the managers schemed to terminate my employment, I soldiered on and, for over three years, I came to work every day on time without having a computer password. I rewrote the documentation for the obsolete computer programs. The Systems Director wrote unhelpful memoranda to me and I wrote back unhelpful replies. I waited patiently either for the EEOC to investigate my complaints or for the Department and its managers to terminate my employment. But the EEOC did not investigate any of my complaints or protect me from the harassment.

In August 1994, the Systems Director wrote to me alleging that my assignments were not complete. He wrote that my previous statement to him, that I am unable to make any improvement, confirmed his belief that I am not capable of providing an acceptable work product. I replied to him that I saw no legitimate reason for him to assign work for me to complete that he did not believe me to be capable of providing. That left him speechless and so I won the memo wars.

CHAPTER FOURTEEN

ASSISTANT COMMISSIONER APPOINTED

So hoist up the John B's sail. See how the main sail sets.
BEACH BOYS.

In June 1992, the Commissioner personally appointed the new Assistant Commissioner for Technical Development and Project Management. He was the first Assistant Commissioner that the Information Systems Division had ever had. He had followed the Commissioner from Crime Victims Board to Probation and then from Probation to Correction. When he arrived at the Department of Correction, the Department brought in interior decorators and carved out one-third of the office space of the Information Systems Division to provide him with a sumptuous and opulent office all of his own; as befitted a gentleman of eminence and accomplishments.

The Assistant Commissioner had a B.A. in English Literature and he had a boating license. His boating skills meant that he knew how to trim a main sail. He could take the helm, navigate the stormy waters and steer the Information Systems Division safely to its destination. However he had never passed a civil service exam, he knew nothing about computer programming and he had never written a computer program. He was always walking up and down the Information

Systems office smoking a cigarette. In July 1992, during his first month with the Department, he set fire to the wastepaper basket.

The Assistant Commissioner straightaway became my immediate supervisor and he took a keen interest in my career. In August 1992, he called me into his office. This is the first time that he spoke to me. He did not invite me to tell him of my complaints of employment discrimination. So what did he say? He told me that there will be no discrimination in his Department but that he will not go beyond the requirements of the law. This was hardly reassuring. He did not void the charges against me or restore my computer password. I believe that the Assistant Commission called me into his office to discourage me from pursuing my complaint of employment discrimination against the Department.

Two days later, the Assistant Commissioner and the Systems Director together harassed me three times in a single day.

First at 9.30 am, the Assistant Commissioner called me into his office. The Systems Director was also in the office. The Assistant Commissioner told me that he had read the Rabbi's letter, and he disagreed with it.

Second at 10.30 am, the Assistant Commissioner called me into his office. The Systems Director was also in the office. The Assistant Commissioner ordered me to have an Inmate Information Systems assignment complete by Friday.

The Department employs Admins to support the IIS. The other computer programmers had been sent on Admins training classes. The Assistant Commissioner told me to learn Admins by reading the manual. I told him that I needed the same Admins training as the other computer programmers had received.

Third at 12.45 pm, he came to my cubicle, together

with the Systems Director, and he asked me how the IIS assignment was getting on.

"I'm trying to work out how I can do it without the training I need."

"Does it concern you that your pacing up and down might disturb fellow employees?"

"Although management has brought me up on charges for pacing, no fellow employee has complained."

"Does it not concern you that your walking about might disturb them?"

"I only concern myself with my work."

"Should you not concern yourself with other employees?"

"If I were to concern myself with other employees, then I would expose myself to disciplinary charges that I do not concern myself exclusively with my work."

"Do you read standing up or sitting down?"

"Sometimes I even read standing on my head."

"Here is an Admins manual. I want you to read it. When you have read it, I want you to report back to me with your questions in writing. Do you understand?"

"Yes."

The Assistant Commissioner and the Systems Director had harassed me three times in one day. I felt threatened and humiliated. The next day when I came into work, I felt so stressed that I only stayed for one hour. I went home again and took a day's sick leave.

The managers treated me differently, and worse, than the other computer programmers. They segregated me from the other computer programmers. The other computer programmers worked under supervision together as a team on the Inmate Information System but the managers isolated me and prohibited me from speaking with co-workers. The law prohibits discrimination against employees by training, but while the other computer programmers were sent on Admins training classes, the managers denied my requests for training and I had been left behind.

The Assistant Commissioner told me to read the Admins manual. He instructed me to work on my own on an IIS assignment and to complete the work by Friday. All of the other computer programmers had computer passwords but the managers had revoked my password. The Assistant Commissioner did not restore my password or send me on the Admins training classes which the other computer programmers had attended. Within two days of his telling me that there will be no discrimination, he was actively participating in the three-year campaign of harassment and discrimination.

Each of us, the Assistant Commissioner and I, had his job to do. If it were his job to intimidate me and to harass me, then it was my job to stay calm, to fend off his attacks, and not allow him to provoke me. Far from going beyond the requirements of the law, the Department and its managers had already fallen short of the law. The three-year campaign of harassment and discrimination had already begun several months ago but the Assistant Commissioner did not take corrective action. He never gave me credit for completing the Visitors Pass system. He had made up his mind to terminate my employment and there was nothing I could say or do that would make any difference. The Union refused to help me. The EEOC did not investigate my complaints.

In November 1992, the Assistant Commissioner called me into a meeting with himself and with the Systems Director. The Assistant Commissioner demanded of me whether I feel an obligation to refrain from misrepresenting and telling lies about the Department. The next day he called me in again to ask me whether I have regard for the truth.

"I did not say 'lies', I asked you whether you had concern for the truth," he said.

"I distinctly remember that you said I was telling 'lies'," I said.

"No, I am concerned for the truth."

"Do you also concern yourself with the constitutional rights of your employees?"

"You can't just go into a crowded cinema and shout fire."

"Congratulations on reading your John Stuart Mill."

"Do you not agree that with rights come responsibilities?"

"I bow to the superior wisdom of my Commissioner."

"How stupid do you think I am?" he asked.

"Stupid enough not to rectify the situation," I replied.

"Oh and Mr. Newman, have a nice day."

"Thank you, Mr. Commissioner, Sir."

The Assistant Commissioner was trying to pick a fight with me. Just as the squid squirts ink to distract predators, so sarcasm is the appropriate employee response to supervisor harassment. The managers goaded me to resign but I continued to come to work every day. I was determined to remain on the job to earn a livelihood and to serve my employer. I waited either for the EEOC to investigate my complaints or for the Department to terminate my employment. It took the managers more than three years to force me to resign.

CHAPTER FIFTEEN

GOOD PEOPLE DID NOTHING

The best lack all conviction while
the worst are full of passionate intensity.
W. B. YEATS.

For evil to flourish, it only requires good men to do nothing.
JOHN STUART MILL.

Brave Sir Robin ran away.
MONTY PYTHON.

The harassment flourished because the Good People did nothing. I needed legal representation. I needed a champion to avenge my legal rights. I approached several law firms that specialize in employment discrimination. I approached several do-good non-profit legal organizations which reach out for tax-deductible charitable donations so that they can continue their good work. Some lawyers wanted to charge me money for consultations. Others were free and generous with good advice and explanations. They liked to play devil's advocate and tell me what the Department of Correction managers were going to say.

The Good People were so wise, intelligent and knowledgeable. They had such valuable insight and they had all the answers at their fingertips. Nobody helped me but everybody had lots of good ideas. They gave me good advice and explanations and they sent me on my way. The more they explained to me, the less they listened to me. The less they listened to me, the less they helped me. The less they helped me, the more the harassment flourished.

I went to several organizations that fight for civil rights, and to several organizations that fight against antisemitism. They collect donations from the public to support the important work that they do. But none of these organizations were willing to help me. The Good People told me that the Correction managers were not nice people and that I would be happier if I got a better job somewhere else. They told me that I was young and I had my health and that was the most important thing.

I complained to the Good People that the managers harassed me. They discriminated against me because I requested accommodation for Sabbath observance. The Good People had the notion that the law did not prohibit harassment; the law only prohibited sexual harassment. They explained to me that the managers could not be antisemitic because they had never said that they hated Jews. Because the managers were not antisemitic, therefore it was all a matter of a personality conflict. If the managers did not accommodate my Sabbath observance, then the reason was that they did not like me. Perhaps they were not satisfied with my work. I must have done something to offend them. The Good People warned me that there was no hope that I could prevail in trial. The Jury would not believe me because the managers had a parade of witnesses to testify against me.

One lawyer explained to me that it was all a misunderstanding. She told me that my supervisor had not agreed to let me leave at 1:00 pm on Friday because he did not understand about Sabbath observance. Once I explain to my supervisor about what Sabbath observance involves, then my supervisor would understand

and then he would let me leave early on Friday, and make up the time, because that is the law.

I used to give money to an organization called the Agudah. In its website, the Agudah claims to be "the leading advocate for the religious and civil rights of observant Jews." I met with the Agudah's attorney. This meeting did not happen straightaway. It took several phone calls and someone interceded on my behalf before he agreed to meet with me. The blue carpeting in the attorney's office was as thick and deep as an ocean and his desk was as solid and imposing as a battleship. I approached his desk, or shall I say I swam aboard, and he asked me how many Jews live in my hometown, and other chat. He said he could not help me as it was my word against the word of my managers. Later on, after I had filed my complaint with the Court, I telephoned him again and this time he said he could not help me as the matter was now in litigation.

The managers intended to terminate my employment and I was frightened. The weight and fury of a City agency bore down upon me for over three years. I needed a champion to litigate my complaint of religious discrimination, to advocate for me in the courtroom, to tell my story to the Jury and to avenge my legal rights. Not one of these Good People stepped forward to be my champion. Instead they gave me good advice.

I came to work every day to present myself to managers who had revoked my computer password and who had brought me up on charges. They were fabricating a case against me. Having revoked my password, they then complained that I did no work. The managers painstakingly created a paper trail of complaints and warnings concerning my behavior and performance. They gave me negative performance evaluations and a corrective interview. Each day might be a day that they would hurl insults at me, humiliate me or try to entrap me into a confrontation in which I could only lose. This abuse went on for more than three years. All I could do was to overcome my fear and to brace myself to come to work each day, to hold on and not resign, to wait patiently either for the EEOC to investigate my complaints or for the Department and its managers to terminate my employment. But the EEOC did not investigate any of my complaints or protect me from the harassment.

The City Personnel Director wrote that my allegations were serious. The City Council President wrote that my allegations were serious. But the Good People told me that it was my word against the word of my managers and that I had no cause for complaint. I persuaded the Arbitrator that I had completed the highly technical Visitors Pass system. I persuaded the Unemployment Benefit Appeal Board that I left my employment for good cause. I persuaded City Corporation Council to settle with me because I had a strong case; yet the Good People did not listen to me.

The Good People bravely turned their back on me. No one listened to me. They gave me no help or encouragement. They would not provide legal representation but they advised me of what I should and should not do. There was no shortage of good advice and the Good People were full of it. They advised me not to resign. When I did resign, they insisted that I had made a mistake. I was on my own. Only my wife stood by me.

Could it be that the Good People would rather collect donations, and apply the money to renting office space and paying salaries, than engage in the hard work of representing a case? I wish that I could take the good advice which the Good People gave to me, place this good advice into a compressor machine and squeeze out a nice small juicy hamburger.

CHAPTER SIXTEEN

CIVIL SERVICE EXAMINATION FOR COMPUTER SPECIALIST SOFTWARE

In November 1991, a promotional examination for the job title of Computer Specialist Software took place. This was more than an internal promotion run by the Department of Correction. This was a citywide civil service promotional examination run by the City Personnel Department.

I had already passed the Civil Service exam for Computer Associate Software. I had been appointed from the civil service list and I had passed probation. I was eligible to apply for this promotional exam. The Systems Director had been appointed from a Staff Analyst list, but not from any computer list. The other managers had not passed any civil service exam at all. None of the managers supervising me were eligible to apply for this promotional exam - neither the Systems Director, the Program Manager, the Executive Director nor the Assistant Commissioner.

I took the exam in November 1991. City Personnel Department was replaced by the Department for Citywide Administrative Services (DCAS). It was not until November 1996 that DCAS notified me that I had passed the exam. According to DCAS, it should only have taken 120 days to mark the exam and to publish the list of candidates who had passed the exam, but it took Personnel and

DCAS five years. Five years! Passing this exam should have been my ticket out of the Department of Correction and promotion into another City agency. I paid good money to apply to take the exam. Five years is too long to wait. By the time the City published the list, I had long resigned from the Department of Correction. It was too late!

I had worked for over four years at the Department as a Computer Associate, and I was due a promotion. For six months, when I worked on the Visitors Pass system, I had already performed the duties of Computer Specialist. I had passed the citywide promotional examination for Computer Specialist. I deserved promotion to Computer Specialist Software, either at the Department of Correction or at another City agency.

In January 1995, the Department transferred me to work in Rikers Island and I resigned. The Unemployment Benefits Appeal Board found that I resigned for good cause and that this was an involuntary resignation. But because I had resigned, promotion was no longer possible. I had left the City payroll and so I was no longer eligible for promotion. I was never called from the promotional list and I never received the promotion which I had paid for and earned.

These managers in the Department of Correction, they were not civil servants themselves, but they had succeeded in derailing my civil service career. I would not have resigned but for the transfer to Rikers Island; and the Department would not have succeeded in transferring me to Rikers Island if the Court had protected me from the transfer and set a trial date. The Court remained silent and it did not uphold the rule of law. The Court enabled the managers to cheat me of my job and my promotion.

CHAPTER SEVENTEEN

PROGRAM MANAGER RESIGNS

Oh, we don't want to lose you,
but we think you ought to go.
PAUL RUBENS.

In January 1990, the Executive Director and the Program Manager interviewed me for a civil service appointment at the Department of Correction. During the interview I informed them that I would need an accommodation to my work schedule to leave at 1:00 pm on Fridays for Sabbath observance but I would make up the time during the rest of the week. They agreed to this arrangement. They selected me from the civil service list and, in April 1990, I reported for work. I was appointed to the Information Systems Division and my immediate supervisor was the Program Manager.

The first year ran smoothly. At that time, I was living in Washington Heights, in northern Manhattan. My commute home was about one hour. The managers accommodated my Sabbath observance. I left at 1:00 pm on Fridays and made up the time by working an hour late on Monday and on Tuesdays. I had a good working relationship with Executive Director Bob Creed and with the Program Manager. Every week, the Executive Director would stop by my cubicle and we would chat for a few minutes. But in March 1991, he became sick. The last time I saw the

Executive Director was in April 1991; when he came into his office wearing his pajamas. He had been my friend. Now I was on my own.

The Program Manager was a competent computer programmer. He was polite and likable. Every day, he used to phone his wife and his married daughter. For my first year, we had a good working relationship. I wrote a series of computer programs used by the Department's Labor Relations unit. In March 1991, he gave me a satisfactory performance evaluation. In April 1991, I passed probation. But also in March or April 1991, my working relationship with the Program Manager seemed to turn sour. This followed the appointment of Raymond Hickox, the new Executive Director.

In March 1991, as the Festival of Passover approached, I gave a box of matzos to the Program Manager. The Program Manager was not Jewish, none of the managers were Jewish, but I gave the matzos to him as a gesture of goodwill. He did not reciprocate the goodwill. There was nothing tangible on the radar but I felt that the atmosphere had become thin. He assigned me to work on the Visitors Pass system. He did not help me with my work so I worked alone without supervision.

In April 1991, I made personal use of the computer to type out an essay for class. There was no Departmental rule that prohibited personal use of the computer. I did not know this at the time, but the Program Manager reported to the Department against me, saying that I had made personal use of the computer. He did not say anything to me about my personal use of the computer. He gave me no warning.

Several months passed and the Program Manager barely spoke to me. I could not understand why he would not speak to me. I always treated him with respect. I was not aware that I had done anything to offend him. Perhaps he was dissatisfied with my work performance? He had no good cause to be dissatisfied; I had completed the highly technical Visitors Pass system.

In October 1991, I went to the Program Manager to request accommodation for Sabbath observance. He told me that he himself did not object but that the Systems Director objected. I went to the new Executive Director. He remained silent. I went to the EEO Officer. She remained silent.

In October 1991, two weeks after I approached the EEO Officer, the Department revoked my computer password. The Department brought three disciplinary charges against me, including that, back in April 1991, I had made personal use of the computer. This charge came as a shock. The charges alleged that I had walked about, that I had made personal use of the computer and that I had raised my voice to my superior, that is, to the Program Manager. In November 1991, the Executive Director held a Step One Conference and he formally presented to the Union the disciplinary charges which he had brought against me.

It became clear that the Program Manager had reported against me and that he was going to testify against me to terminate my employment with the Department. He was going to get me fired. The outlook was bleak and it appeared that I was about to lose my job. But there was hope. The Department's case against me rested upon the testimony of the Program Manager. Perhaps my employment would not be terminated if the Program Manager were to resign.

There is a City rule that all employees must reside within the City unless they have been granted a waiver. The Program Manager had not been granted a waiver and he was living at an address outside of the City. Moreover there is a City rule that any City employee who knows of anyone breaking any of the rules has an affirmative duty to vigilantly report it to the Department of Investigation.

People who live in glass houses should not throw stones. According to the Telephone Directory White Pages, his driving license and his voting record, these are all public records, the Program Manager was living at an address outside of the City; and this was contrary to the City's rules that require City employees to reside within the City. The Program Manager had been recruited from the Mayor's Talent Bank. He did not have a college degree, he had not passed any civil service examination and he was not protected by Civil Service law.

In November 1991, I reported to the Inspector General that the Program Manager had violated the City's residency requirement. The reason why I reported the Program Manager was to save my job. He had already reported against me to get me fired. Now I reported against him to get him fired. He started this and I struck back.

The Inspector General took no action and so, in February 1992, I wrote to the Commissioner for Investigation concerning the Program Manager. Also in February 1992, I requested my City Council Member to follow up with the Department of Investigation and to remind the Department to investigate whether the Program Manager had violated the City's residency requirement.

In May 1992, the Department of Investigation began its investigation into the residency of the Program Manager. It was rumored that the Program Manager met with the Commissioner for Correction and they discussed promoting him to a job title where City residency is not required. The Commissioner promised him that she would try to hold off the investigation. In May 1992, the Program Manager gave me a negative performance evaluation. In his evaluation of my performance, he called me a troublemaker and he recommended terminating my employment. A few days after giving me a negative performance evaluation, the Program Manager stood at the opening of my cubicle and he told me that I was a dead man.

The Department and its managers needed the Program Manager to be a witness against me. They had to prioritize their efforts between protecting the Program Manager from the Department of Investigation, and terminating my employment. The Commissioner for Correction did not protect the Program Manager and he was not granted a waiver of the residency requirement.

From April 1990 until April 1991, I had a good working relationship with the Program Manager. In April 1991, the first Executive Director left the Department and a second Executive Director was appointed. I believe that the Systems Director incited the Program Manager against me. The Program Manager was a fool to listen and this mistake cost him his job. By May 1992, after the Department for Investigation had begun its inquiry, the Program Manager had become a backward pawn in the game. In June 1992, the second Executive Director told me that from now on I was to report directly to the Systems Director.

In August 1992, the Program Manager resigned. He was not replaced. The Systems Director said that the Program Manager was a good employee and that I had done wrong to cause him to lose his job, when he was at the end of his career.

The Program Manager had threatened my employment. I had to do whatever was necessary and reasonable in order to remain employed. There is the City rule about reporting wrongdoing to the Department of Investigation and so I had reported the Program Manager's residency outside New York City. But the reason

I did this was that he had caused charges to be brought against me. Had it not been for the charges, then I would not have reported the Program Manager to the Inspector General or to the Commissioner for Investigation. I would have remained silent in the face of the Program Manager's violation of the code of residency. My vigilancy would have been sorely lacking.

In December 1992, the managers took the Program Manager out for dinner. It was rumored that they asked him to testify against me in the upcoming civil service disciplinary hearing, but he refused. A co-worker had signed a statement to say that he witnessed that I had raised my voice to the Program Manager. The co-worker now repudiated his statement against me. He swore an affidavit denying that he had heard me raise my voice to the Program Manager. The co-worker swore that he had signed his previous statement against me because he had been told to do so by the Program Manager. So now the Department had no witnesses to produce against me. This raised my hope that I could emerge unscathed from the disciplinary hearing.

CHAPTER EIGHTEEN

DISCIPLINARY CHARGES ARE ADJOURNED CONTEMPLATING DISMISSAL

We shall go on to the end, we shall fight on the beaches, we shall fight in the hills; we shall never surrender.
WINSTON CHURCHILL.

Gonna stand my ground and I won't back down.
TOM PETTY.

The mission of OATH's Trials Division is to provide fair and neutral administrative proceedings, which protect the due process rights of all litigants. Matters adjudicated at the Trials Division are akin to civil trials without a jury...The administrative law judge will preside over the hearing in a fair and impartial manner. OATH Statement.

In New York City, the managers cannot terminate the employment of permanent civil servants at will. Disciplinary charges have to be served and there has to be a civil service disciplinary hearing before the Office of Administrative Trials and Hearings ("OATH") which provides for an impartial judge. On October 23, 1991, the Executive Director served me with disciplinary charges. The charges had three specifications. First, I had raised my voice to my supervisor, second, I had made personal use of the computer and third, I had walked about. The same day as he served me with charges, he also revoked my computer password.

In October 8, 1991, I approached the EEO Officer to request accommodation for Sabbath observance. Two weeks later, on October 23, 1991, the managers revoked my computer password and brought me up on charges. Because of the close proximity in time, I believe that the managers revoked my password and served the charges to retaliate because I had requested accommodation for Sabbath observance.

On October 23, 1991, the Executive Director served me with charges and, on November 27, 1991, he held a Step One Conference in which he presented these charges to the Union. This Conference was held pursuant to the Union-City Collective Bargaining Agreement. The Executive Director recommended that I would be suspended without pay from my employment for forty-five days, fifteen days for each charge. The Union Representative said forty-five days is too long for a first offense and it violates the principle of progressive discipline. There was little discussion. This was a formalistic ritual presentation of charges. The meeting lasted for only a few minutes.

I had not broken any rule but the Union Representative was too eager to plead me guilty. My job was under threat. If I wanted to keep my job, then I simply could not afford to plead guilty, or pay any penalty at all. The managers were determined to terminate my employment. Guilt and innocence had nothing to do with it. The managers were never going to leave me in peace. If I were found guilty of misconduct, or if I paid any penalty whatsoever, even just a slap on the wrist, then this would undermine my morale, compromise my innocence and encourage the Department to bring more and more charges against me in the ensuing weeks and months until my employment would be terminated. There could be no retreat. I had to go on to the end. I had to stand my ground. I could not take one step back.

According to the Union grievance procedure, once the Step One Conference had been held, a Step Two Conference became due. But I had met with the Department of Correction's Deputy Commissioner for Trials and she had recommended that, rather than follow the Union disciplinary grievance procedure, I should defend myself before OATH in a civil service disciplinary hearing. I followed her advice and I demanded from the Union that OATH should hold the hearing. The Union retained an attorney to represent me at the hearing. OATH provides for an evidentiary hearing, with an impartial judge, cross-examination of witnesses and a written record.

Civil Service law provides that no permanent civil servant shall be terminated or subjected to disciplinary penalty except for incompetency or misconduct after a hearing upon stated charges. Civil Service hearings are held by OATH. The Administrative Law Judge hears the charge brought by the City agency against a civil servant. Once the charge has been heard, then the Judge makes a recommendation to the Commissioner and then the Commissioner makes a decision. The Commissioner's decision can be appealed to the Civil Service Commission or to the Court.

Because OATH is independent of the City agency that brings the charge, then the employee can reasonably hope that the hearing will fairly seek out the truth and provide for due process. The hearing proceeds as a civil trial and the civil servant can expect an impartial judge who will weigh the evidence. OATH is a charter agency of the City of New York.

It employs administrative law judges and it conducts administrative hearings.

OATH emulates a civil court; but it is not a court. It cannot impose imprisonment and the standard of proof is preponderance of the evidence, not beyond reasonable doubt. The City agency can bring disciplinary charges against the employee for violating Department Rules but the employee cannot go to OATH to bring charges against his agency or against his supervisor. If the employee chooses to bring charges, then he has to go to Court. This is just as well because, if the employee does go to Court, then he can demand a Jury and ask for compensatory and punitive damages.

In April 1993, a preliminary pre-trial OATH Conference took place in an OATH courtroom. There were five people in the room. I came to the Conference accompanied by my wife and by my defense attorney. The Prosecutor represented the Department of Correction. The Judge chaired the Conference. The Department had charged me with raising my voice to my supervisor, making personal use of the computer and walking about. Two years had elapsed since I had made personal use of the computer.

I told the Judge my answer to the charges. It was untrue that I had raised my voice to my supervisor. It was true that I had walked about but I deserved credit for having completed the Visitors Pass system. It was true that I had made personal use of the computer, but there was no rule in the Department's Rules and Regulations that prohibits an employee from making personal use of the computer, nor had there been any warning. I told the Judge, the real reason why the Department brought the charges was that I had requested accommodation for Sabbath observance.

The Prosecutor did not dispute either my facts or

my interpretation. The Judge listened to what I had to say, she treated me with dignity and she succeeded in mediating a resolution to the Department's charges against me. No one in the room wanted this case to go to trial and within an hour we reached a plea agreement by which the charges were adjourned contemplating dismissal. This plea agreement was without prejudice to my pending litigation against the Department.

If I were innocent, then why agree to a plea agreement, why not let the case go to trial? The managers wanted to fire me. Who knows but if the case were to come to trial, then the Judge might find me guilty of personal use of the computer. Then the managers would make further efforts to fire me in future proceedings. Because of the plea agreement, I accomplished my objective; to pay no penalty and to admit no guilt. I had stopped the charges dead in their tracks.

I emerged from the ordeal of the charges without a scratch. I won and the managers lost. The Deputy Commissioner for Trials had kept her word. I had not been suspended for a single day, not even for one hour. I had not received any token punishment, I had paid no penalty whatsoever, I had admitted no guilt and the proceedings were over. All that had happened was that the Department of Correction had agreed to expunge the charges in six months unless new charges were served. I beat the rap.

That very same day, the second Executive Director was fired. The managers were in disarray. They had attempted to terminate my employment and they had failed. They had brought charges against me but they had not secured a conviction. They had lost momentum and prestige. They had not managed to make the charges stick. Instead the managers had egg sticking to their face. They did not dare bring any new charges.

A NEGOTIATED PLEA AGREEMENT FOR SETTLEMENT OF DISCIPLINARY MATTERS WITHIN THE DEPARTMENT OF CORRECTION

Prior to the commencement of plea negotiations, it is acknowledged as hereinafter subscribed by the Respondent, Respondent's Attorney and the Department's Trial Division, that any subsequent agreement concerning a stipulated penalty which may be accepted by the Trial Division will constitute the Trial Division's recommendation to the Commissioner of Correction.

In the event that plea negotiations do not result in an agreement, no statements by the Respondent or his Attorney in connection and relevant thereto, will be admissible against the Respondent. The Respondent's rights and privileges, including the right to an Administrative Hearing will remain unaffected, and the Department's Disciplinary process will proceed as if plea negotiations had never taken place.

Respondent further warrants that any supporting documents or affidavits submitted by Respondent in connection with or for the purpose of inducing the Department to accept this negotiated plea, are truthful. In the event said documents are proven to be inaccurate or false, you will be subjected to additional charges and the plea agreement will become null and void.

Date: 4/19/93 — C S Newman 29133
Signature, I.D./~~Shield~~#

Law Office of L. Jack Goldstoff
BY: Michelle Jacobowitz, Esq.
Attorney for Respondent

Attorney/Trial Division

In the matter of the INFORMAL CONFERENCE held for

CYRIL Steve Newman of the Department of Correction, holding the position of

Computer Associate Shield ______, Institution: Information Services :

I, CYRIL Steve Newman, acknowledge receipt of a copy of the charges and specifications ~~dated~~ served 10/23/91, OATH No ~~DR~~#(s) 509/93, and annexed thereto.

I am fully aware of the fact that I am entitled to a disciplinary Hearing pursuant to section 75 of the Civil Service Law in which I would be entitled to representation, to confront witnesses against me and to present witnesses on my behalf. I am also aware that I may elect to appeal an adverse decision rendered after such hearing to either the Supreme Court of the State of New York or the Civil Service Commissioner in accordance with procedures set forth in Section 76 of the Civil Service Law.

I have been advised that ~~the penalty~~ recommended for the charges and specifications sustained against me is as follows:

1) The above charges in addition to any outstanding or potential charges to date, are hereby Adjourned contemplating Dismissal for a period of six months. 2) Should no new charges be brought during the six month period the above charges are to be expunged from Mr. Newman's disciplinary history. 3) This settlement is without prejudice to any other pending litigation matter brought by Mr. Newman.

If this ~~penalty~~ is approved by the Commissioner of Correction, I accept said decision, and as a condition of accepting such decision of the Commissioner of Correction, I hereby waive any and all rights granted to me under section 75 and 76 of the Civil Service Law and ~~acknowledge that this acceptance is the same as a finding of guilt after a hearing~~.

~~I am fully aware that if the Commissioner of Correction approves the penalty, this waiver of my right to a section 75 hearing is final and irrevocable and that this waiver will be placed in my permanent personnel file, as a disposition of the Disciplinary Charges and specifications. Further, I fully understand that the Commissioner may reduce the penalty at his or her own discretion and I hereby consent to such reduction.~~

~~I acknowledge the Commissioner at his or her discretion may reduce said penalty, without respondents reappearance.~~

~~This agreement includes a period of probation, (Attached Form #______)~~ ______ ~~initials.~~

______ Action by Commissioner of Corrections ______ Approved.

~~Penalty reduced as follows:~~ ______

C S Newman
4/19/93
Dated

Law Office of L. Jack Goldstoff
BY: Michelle Jacobowitz, Esq.
Attorney for Respondent

Attorney/Trial Division

I hereby approve the ~~penalty~~ recommended herein.

Ronald A. Gregg
Acting Assistant Commissioner,
Trials and Litigation

Catherine M. Abate
Commissioner of Correction

EXHIBIT 7. *Plea agreement for charges to be adjourned, dated April 19, 1993.*

CHAPTER NINETEEN

SECOND EXECUTIVE DIRECTOR IS FIRED

We cannot all be masters,
nor all masters cannot be truly follow'd.
SHAKESPEARE.

And hast thou slain the Jabberwock?
Come to my arms, my beamish boy!
LEWIS CARROLL.

I reported for work in April 1990. When I first interviewed for the position, the Executive Director and Program Manager agreed to an accommodation by which I could leave on Friday afternoons at 1:00 pm for Sabbath observance and make up the time. In March 1991, Executive Director Bob Creed became sick and, in April 1991, he left the Department. In March 1991, Raymond Hickox was appointed Executive Director. He replaced Bob Creed.

In April 1991, Executive Director Hickox called me into his office. He told me that I am obnoxious. He canceled the accommodation for Sabbath observance that Bob Creed had approved. He told me that I had to leave at 4:00 pm on Fridays as he did not approve of employees working irregular hours. He threatened to bring me up on disciplinary charges if I did not complete the Visitors Pass system.

In October 1991, I approached Executive Director Hickox to request accommodation for Sabbath observance but he remained silent. I approached the EEO Officer to request accommodation for Sabbath observance but she remained silent. Two weeks later, the Executive Director revoked my computer password and he served charges upon me. In November 1991, he held a Step One Conference and he presented the charges to the Union.

In December 1992, the managers took the Program Manager out to dinner but he had resigned and they could not get him to testify against me. In March 1993, the Executive Director spoke to me in the men's room. The two of us had not spoken for months. He told me that he wanted to reintegrate me into the Department. What? The disciplinary hearing was scheduled to take place next month. The Executive Director wanted to reach an agreement but he came empty-handed and I sensed that he was about to lose his job. He had nothing to trade, he had done me nothing but harm and his overture was too late. I was confident that I could emerge from the hearing unscathed and so I did not crave any agreement or favor from the Executive Director.

"Two years ago you threatened to bring charges and fire me. I'm still here," I said.

"The charges are still standing."

"But you can't make them stick."

"You want to play that game? I'll make them stick," he said.

What goes around, comes around. The Executive Director had brought me up on charges; but he could not make the charges stick, and his goose was cooked. He had not passed any civil service examination and he was not protected by Civil Service law. The OATH pre-trial conference took place in April 1993 and the charges were adjourned contemplating dismissal. That very same day, the Executive Director was fired. He had been the Executive Director of the Information Systems Division for exactly two years, from April 1991 until April 1993. The Assistant Commissioner stomped upon the Executive Director as pitilessly as the Executive Director had stomped upon the cockroach. In May 1993, the Executive Director's wife divorced him. It never rains, but it pours.

In October 1991, when the second Executive Director served the disciplinary charges, he also revoked my computer password. In April 1993, the charges were adjourned contemplating dismissal but the managers still did not restore my password. I was employed by the Department as a computer programmer yet I still came to work every day without a password. With the Program Manager gone and with the second Executive Director gone, and with the charges adjourned, I might have hoped that my password would be restored. I might have hoped for some peace and to be allowed to get on with my job. But no, the Department appointed a third Executive Director and the managers regrouped for a fresh assault. The managers continued their three-year campaign of harassment and discrimination against me and they intended to terminate my employment.

In June 1993, Systems Director Waldmann recommended new disciplinary charges for the third Executive Director to bring against me. There were four pages of new charges. The charges alleged that I had raised my voice to my new supervisor, this is the junior employee who had attempted to assign work duties to me, that I had saluted the Systems Director and that I had told the Systems Director not to read the newspaper. The prosecutor assured me that these new charges were mickey mouse charges that were not going anywhere. During legal discovery, the City Corporation Counsel provided me with a copy of the Systems Director's new charges. Perhaps these new charges had been placed in my personnel file, but they were never served upon me.

PART THREE

THREE-YEAR CAMPAIGN OF HARASSMENT

CHAPTER TWENTY

THE ASSISTANT COMMISSIONER BRANDS ME INCOMPETENT

The printed list of the Chess Committee
was one name shorter. Syme had never existed.
ORWELL.

In May 1992, the Program Manager told me that I was a dead man. In November 1992, Systems Director Waldmann prohibited me from speaking with co-workers. In March 1993, a list was circulated of authorized users of computer passwords but my name was not included in the list.

The managers had ostracized me and they had made me feel that I was not a part of the Information Systems Division. I was an unperson. The managers did not allow me to speak with my co-workers and the co-workers were not allowed to speak with me. Nevertheless one co-worker did dare to speak with me. She told me that she had been instructed not to speak with me but that she was going to speak with me anyway. My wife and I took her out for dinner.

In May 1993, the Information Systems Division held an office party. An attendance list was circulated and the staff were invited by name. But my name was not included in the list and I was not invited to come to the party. Dead men do not need computer passwords, nor do they get invited to office parties. The managers had revoked my computer password and Systems Director Waldmann did not give me computer programming work to do. Instead he gave me the sham make-work duties of documenting obsolete computer programs. He wrote hostile and belligerent memoranda to me and to others about me.

In May 1993, the Systems Director attempted to demote me. A new computer programmer had just been hired. The Systems Director instructed me to report to this junior employee as my new supervisor. I was a permanent tenured civil servant, a computer programmer with three years of seniority, I had completed the Visitors Pass system and I had performed the duties of a Computer Specialist. I deserved a commendation. This junior employee had not passed any civil service examination and he had no seniority, but he attempted to assign work duties to me. Under Civil Service law, the Systems Director could not formally demote me without first holding a disciplinary hearing.

My salary remained unchanged but, without any disciplinary hearing, the Systems Director presented me with a situation that was tantamount to a demotion. If I were to accept work duties from a junior employee, then this would ratify the demotion. The Systems Director wrote charges saying that I raised my voice to my superior, that is, to this junior employee, but the charges were never served.

In June 1993, the Systems Director raised his voice and shouted at me and he called me incompetent and crazy. No one had ever before called me incompetent. I had completed the Visitors Pass system and here comes the Systems Director calling me incompetent and crazy! Them's fighting words. The Systems Director shouting at me was a part of the three-year campaign of harassment. I was already accustomed to being mistreated. It was to be expected. But this was the first time that any supervisor had alleged incompetency and this is the first time that any supervisor had ever raised his voice to me.

I immediately went to see the Assistant Commissioner in his office to complain. The Assistant Commissioner told me that he was very busy. I told him that the Systems Director had called me incompetent and crazy. The Assistant Commissioner asked whether there were any witnesses and I said there were none. He told me that there was nothing that he could do and he did not reprimand the Systems Director or take corrective action. This was June 1993 and this was to be the last time that the Assistant Commissioner and I spoke to each other. The next day, a co-worker came to me and he told me that he had witnessed the Systems Director shouting at me.

I grieved to the City Labor Relations Director that the Systems Director had shouted at me. The City Labor Relations Director replied that my complaint was not grievable within the Collective Bargaining Agreement. In May 1992, the Commissioner for Correction had published her policy that she expected vigorous efforts to create a workplace environment where everybody is treated with dignity. In June 1993, I wrote directly to the Commissioner to complain that the Systems Director had shouted at me. The Commissioner did not reply. The Systems Director shouted at me with impunity that I am incompetent and crazy. Where is the dignity in that? The Department did not put into effect the policy that employees are to be treated with dignity. Nor did the Department have an effective policy for reporting and resolving complaints.

I complained to the EEOC that the Systems Director shouted at me. The EEOC did not investigate this or any of my other complaints. The law says that employees have a right to work in an environment free from discriminatory intimidation, ridicule, and insult. ("Vinson"). No one protected me from the Systems Director shouting at me.

In July 1993, the Assistant Commissioner wrote a two-page memorandum about me to the Commissioner. He wrote that I was a major disruptive force, that I had done absolutely no work and that I was actively attempting to undermine the effectiveness of the Department. He wrote that I exploited the well meant attempts by many managers to work with me, that I had been the subject of numerous disciplinary hearings, charges etc and that I had managed to avoid sanctions by using technical loopholes and manipulating the legal processes. He recommended to the Commissioner that I was incompetent and that he was resuming action against me. The Assistant Commissioner did not provide me with a copy of this memorandum. The City Corporation Counsel gave me a copy during legal discovery.

In October 1991, I approached the EEO Officer. Two weeks later, the managers retaliated. They revoked my computer password and this prevented me from doing my job. There was a three-year campaign of harassment and retaliation. They denied me training and they gave me sham make-work duties. They served me with disciplinary charges but the charges were adjourned contemplating dismissal. They gave me negative performance evaluations and a corrective interview.

Because the managers revoked my password, I could not do my job. Because I could not do my job, the Assistant Commissioner told the Commissioner that I was incompetent. He wrote that I had done absolutely no work and that he intended to resume action against me. Under Civil Service law, no disciplinary penalty may be taken against a civil servant except for incompetency or misconduct. But without any hearing, the Assistant Commissioner called me incompetent and he transferred me to Rikers Island.

The three charges brought against me in October 1991 alleged that I had raised my voice to my supervisor, that I had made personal use of the computer and that I had walked about; these are charges of misconduct. But in all the excitement, the managers forgot to bring a fourth charge. They should have alleged that I was incompetent and that I did absolutely no work. Perhaps the managers had run out of ink. Or perhaps they did not sincerely believe that I was incompetent.

TD #2

THE CITY OF NEW YORK
DEPARTMENT OF CORRECTION
60 HUDSON STREET
NEW YORK, N.Y. 10013-4393

CATHERINE M. ABATE
COMMISSIONER

RICHARD SHAPI
ASSISTANT COMMISSI
TECHNICAL DEVELOPM

RECEIVED
1993
EQUAL EMPLOYMENT OPPORTUNITY OFFICE

TO: Catherine M. Abate, Commissioner;

VIA: Edward J. Allocco, Deputy Commissioner

FROM: Richard B. Shapiro, Assistant Commissioner for Technical Development

RE: **Cyril "Steve" Newman**

DATE: July 1, 1993

Regarding your memo of June 28th, OCA 93/1787, regarding the status of this situation, please consider the following:

Mr. Newman did in fact approach me in the hallway, and state that Mr. Waldmann had called him incompetent and crazy. Mr. Newman is incorrect in stating that he alleged that Mr. Waldmann raised his voice. Mr. Newman is also incorrect in stating that I did nothing. In fact, I interviewed Mr. Newman, asking him about the circumstances of the conversation and whether or not there were any witnesses. Mr. Newman was not responsive to my questions, except insofar as to state that there were no witnesses. I followed up that same day with Mr. Waldmann. Mr. Waldmann stated that he did not call Mr. Newman crazy, but that he did question Mr. Newman's competence. I concur with Mr. Waldmann's characterization of Mr. Newman as incompetent.

Mr. Cyril "Steve" Newman is a major disrupting force in the Information Services Division workplace. Since my arrival here over one year ago, Mr. Newman has done absolutely no work, has managed to disrupt workers, and is actively attempting to undermine the effectiveness of the Division and the Department. All attempts to rectify this situation have met with failure. how?

Mr. Newman has been the subject of numerous disciplinary hearings, charges, etc. He has managed to avoid sanctions by using technical loopholes and by manipulating the legal processes. He has exploited the well meant attempts by many managers to work with him, give him direction, abide by due process, etc.

B0020

EXHIBIT 8. *Assistant Commissioner tells Commissioner that I am incompetent, dated July 1, 1993.*

Mr. Newman is insubordinate and exhibits behavior which is not suitable for an office workplace. He constantly paces up and down the hallways within the work area. Constantly means that he paces for upwards of six hours a day, five days a week. While he paces, he talks to himself aloud, or makes comments to others. Occasionally his comments are rude or nonsensical. From time to time, he likes to salute people. When asked about his behavior, he says that he is thinking. When asked what he is thinking about, he says that it is none of anyone's business. When directed to stop pacing, he usually returns to his desk for a nap. When awakened, he denies sleeping. After a nap, he resumes pacing. This has been going on for many months, and I am informed that it began before I got here.

Over a year ago, Mr. Newman filed an complaint of anti-semitism against this Department. According to Ms. Patricia Mulligan, a probable cause finding was rendered, due to the incorrect handling of the complaint by this agency. During the time which the finding was in place, we were informed by Acting Assistant Commissioner Ronald Gregg that we could take no disciplinary actions of any kind against Mr. Newman. As we have been informed that the probable cause action has been removed, actions are resuming against him now. I believe that his memo to you and Assistant Commissioner Yates is meant to attempt to anticipate the new charges against him.

You should be aware that at no time during my entire time here, am I aware of any mistreatment of Mr. Newman in any way, and especially as regards Mr. Newman's alleged religious requirements. We have ensured that Mr. Newman is allowed to leave several hours early each Friday to observe the Sabbath, even though during the summer hours, when sundown is much later in the day, this should not be necessary. We have approved Mr. Newman's requests for time off for every religious holiday. Further, I have made it extremely clear to all managers and supervisors and all other employees in the Division's under my supervision, that all employee's will be totally respected as to their rights to practice their religions.

Mr. Newman is distracting managers, upsetting co-workers, and consuming a very large amount of everyone's time in the process. I am convening a meeting to discuss our rights and alternatives regarding this matter, to include A.C. Yates, Acting A.C. Gregg, the Equal Employment Office of this agency, and the Legal Division. I will advise you of the outcome of this meeting.

C: Robert Daly, Special Counsel
Richard Yates, Assistant Commissioner
Ronald Gregg, Acting Assistant Commissioner
Patricia Mulligan, Director, EEO

B00203

EXHIBIT 8. *Continued.*

CHAPTER TWENTY-ONE

NEGATIVE PERFORMANCE EVALUATIONS

Either this man is dead or my watch has stopped.
GROUCHO MARX.

If she weighs the same as a duck, then she's made of wood, and therefore she's a witch.
MONTY PYTHON.

What need we fear who knows it, when none can call our power to account?
SHAKESPEARE.

In February 1990, I was appointed from the civil service list for Computer Associate Software to the Information Systems Division of the Department of Correction. In April 1990, I reported for work. In March 1991, the Program Manager gave me a satisfactory performance evaluation. In April 1991, I completed probation.

In March 1991, the Program Manager instructed me to develop the Visitors Pass system. In September 1991, I completed the Visitors Pass system. In October 1991, I approached the Department's EEO Officer to request accommodation for Sabbath observance. Two weeks later, the managers retaliated. They brought me up on disciplinary charges and they revoked my computer password. In December 1991, I complained to the EEOC.

The managers engaged in a three-year campaign of harassment and discrimination. This campaign against me included the writing of two negative performance evaluations, one in May 1992 written by the Program Manager, and one in July 1993 written by the Systems Director and by the Executive Director. Clearly the managers were creating a paper trail to show that they were not satisfied with my performance. Perhaps the performance evaluations were intended for my benefit. Perhaps I should have worked harder and made more effort. Or maybe I was incompetent? Maybe the managers gave me negative performance evaluations because I properly deserved to be given negative performance evaluations? Stuff and nonsense!

In May 1992, the Program Manager gave me a five-page negative performance evaluation. He evaluated me as a probationary employee but this is not correct. I was not a probationary employee. I had completed my probation in April 1991, one year before the evaluation was written. When he gave me the evaluation saying that I was a probationary employee, I was already a permanent tenured civil servant. The Program Manager, however, had not served any probation. Nor had he passed any civil service examination.

The evaluation was too focused on listing my personality flaws. It said *"Mr. Newman lacks initiative and leadership. He is insubordinate. He has a very bad attitude which I consider as that of a troublemaker."* The Program Manager's evaluation of my performance did not mention that I had completed the Visitors Pass system. Instead, he recommended terminating my employment.

There is a City rule that all employees must reside within the City. The Program Manager did not reside within the City. He should not have been employed by the City. It is axiomatic that a person, who should not have been employed by the City, should not then have supervised me or have written my performance evaluation. In May 1992, the Program Manager gave me a negative performance evaluation. He resigned in August 1992, three months later. But the damage was done. A performance evaluation once written is set in stone. It cannot be reviewed, appealed or grieved.

In July 1993, one of the secretaries came to my cubicle and she told me that she needed my help. I followed her and she led me to the Systems Director's office. There were three people in the office, the Systems Director, the third Executive Director, and the junior employee. The secretary had attempted to lure me into an ambush. I left the System Director's office and I returned to my cubicle. She returned a few minutes later and she told me that I was needed for my performance evaluation. I returned to the office and I told the Systems Director that I would not receive my performance evaluation in the presence of a junior employee. I left the office and I returned to my cubicle. A few minutes later, the secretary called me back into the Systems Director's office. The junior employee had left the office. The Systems Director and the Executive Director then gave me the performance evaluation. So ended the attempt of the Systems Director to demote me.

Systems Director Waldmann gave me a negative performance evaluation. This evaluation was three pages long yet it did not mention the Visitors Pass system. It stated that my overall rating was unsatisfactory. *"Mr. Newman has not completed any assignments... He had to be told to redo the work several times... Mr. Newman's performance has been unacceptable by any reasonable standard... Mr. Newman has resisted all efforts to improve his work... I am recommending immediate termination."* The third Executive Director endorsed the evaluation.

The managers wrote that I had not completed any assignments. However, the Visitors Pass system was a highly technical assignment which I completed without help from my supervisor. The managers were municipal government officials and they exercised authority vested in them by the City of New York. They abused their authority by issuing official documents which were false and misleading. The real reason why they gave me negative performance evaluations is that I had requested accommodation for Sabbath observance.

Neither Systems Director Waldmann, Executive Director Hickox nor the Assistant Commissioner had ever passed a civil service computer examination, nor had any of them ever written a computer program. The physician's evaluation of the patient is founded upon empirical evidence and only a licensed physician may practice medicine. But the supervisor's evaluation of the employee is entirely subjective. Civil Service law does not require the supervisor to have passed a civil service examination. A supervisor is not required to know computer programming to supervise a computer programmer.

Why performance evaluations? Supervisors have traditionally enjoyed wide discretion and latitude when writing evaluations of the performance of employees. Are performance evaluations laudatory? It depends on whether they are positive evaluations or negative evaluations. Positive performance evaluations are laudatory because they inform the employee of what management expects, how the employee measures up, and what he or she needs to do to obtain wage increases, promotions or other recognition.

The performance evaluation is shaped entirely by the perception of the supervisor and the supervisor is relying upon his authority and he is exercising his discretion as supervisor. Absent a clear path to challenge and appeal a negative evaluation before an impartial factfinder, then a negative performance evaluation cannot be tested or validated. Negative performance evaluations are a manifestation of raw power by the supervisor over the employee. The law says that a performance evaluation does not have to be fair or even correct. But if an evaluation is not correct, then it serves no purpose. It is like a clock that does not tell the time.

Some employers may have procedures for appealing performance evaluations but the Department of Correction did not have an evaluation appeals procedure. I complained to the Union about the negative performance evaluations. The Union Representative explained to me that the evaluations proved that my supervisors were not satisfied with my work. I wrote an appeal to the Personnel Director. He did not reply.

Negative performance evaluations do not benefit the employee. Courts do not entertain standalone complaints of negative performance evaluations. No court sits to arbitrate mere differences of opinion between employees and their supervisors. There are no safeguards to check that the evaluations are wise, fair, or even correct. The supervisor can spew venom at an employee and make offensive and untruthful comments while leaving the employee with no remedy. A negative performance evaluation is invidious when the civil servant has passed the civil service examination and the supervisor has not passed the civil service examination. Negative performance evaluations cause embarrassment and emotional distress to employees. They undermine employee morale and they lead to low self-esteem. They pave the path to terminating an employee. Negative performance evaluations discourage employees from making complaints of employment discrimination.

What does the law say? One court says that evaluating employees is laudable and should be encouraged because it benefits the employee. ("Jensen"). A second court says that it is only the perception of the manager that matters and the court does not consider whether the performance evaluation is wise, fair, or even correct. ("Hawkins"). A third court says that a supervisor is not required to like his employees. ("Williams"). Yet a fourth court says that negative performance evaluations discourage employees from complaining of employment discrimination ("Vega").

Under the law, a negative performance evaluation is not a disciplinary action that needs a hearing. Nor is it an adverse action which affects the terms and conditions of employment. A negative performance evaluation is neither fish nor flesh and an employee knows not where to have it. Civil Service law calls a negative performance evaluation an "adverse personnel action." But there is no legal requirement for the supervisor to give to the employee a performance evaluation that is wise, fair and correct. There is no opportunity for the employee to appeal the evaluation or to dispute the evaluation before an impartial hearing officer.

After giving me the evaluation, the Systems Director then wrote to the Assistant Commissioner and recommended dismissing me from my employment. The Systems Director then wrote to me saying the fact that I had received a negative performance evaluation proved that I was incompetent. The Assistant Commissioner recommended to the Commissioner that I am incompetent. The managers clearly intended to terminate my employment.

I complained to the EEOC that the negative performance evaluations were given to retaliate because I had approached the EEO Officer to request accommodation for Sabbath observance. But the EEOC did not investigate any of my complaints or protect me from the harassment. I complained to the Court but the Court sat on my complaint and it did not set a trial date. There was no remedy.

This was to be the last day that I met face to face with the Systems Director. Eighteen months passed and no further performance evaluations were given to me. The Assistant Commissioner recommended to the Commissioner that I was incompetent and that he was taking action against me. Then he transferred me to Rikers Island.

He has spent excessive time conversing with others, and through his insubordination, refusal to work, hostile attitude, daily pacing the hallway, absence from his desk, sleeping at his desk, and reading non-work-related material, has been a poor example to other workers. In addition, he has projected an unacceptable image to other divisions of the Department.

2. The employee's overall rating is:

1. ____ Unratable
2. __X__ Unsatisfactory
3. ____ Conditional
3. ____ Satisfactory
4. ____ Superior
5. ____ Outstanding

Justification for overall rating.

In his work and in other performance factors not included in the tasks, Mr. Newman's performance has been unacceptable by any reasonable standard.

C. PLANS AND RECOMMENDATIONS

1. Plans to improve employee's performance:

None Mr. Newman has resisted all efforts to improve his work and behavior. I am recommending immediate termination of Mr. Newman's employment.

2. Plans and recommendations to capitalize upon employee's strengths:

None Mr. Newman has resisted all efforts to change. I am recommending immediate termination.

3. Plans to change conditions:

I am recommending immediate termination.

D. RECORD OF APPRAISAL INTERVIEW

EMPLOYEE'S SIGNATURE ____ DATE ____

[signature] SUPERVISOR'S SIGNATURE — DATE 7/15/93

[signature] REVIEWER'S SIGNATURE — DATE 7/15/93

Mr. Newman refused to sign this performance evaluation.

EXHIBIT 9. *Performance evaluation recommending termination of employment, dated July 15, 1993.*

THE CITY OF NEW YORK
DEPARTMENT OF CORRECTION
60 HUDSON STREET
NEW YORK, N.Y. 10013-4393

CATHERINE M. ABATE
COMMISSIONER

RICHARD SHAPIRO
ASSISTANT COMMISSIONER
TECHNICAL DEVELOPMENT

TO: Valentino Johnson, Section Supervisor, Classification, Evaluation & Programs

FROM: Doug Waldmann, Director, Systems Development

DATE: July 16, 1993

SUBJECT: SUB-MANAGERIAL PERFORMANCE EVALUATION - CYRIL NEWMAN

Attached please find Cyril (Steve) Newman's Task & Standards along with his evaluation. I,am strongly recommending Mr. Newman's immediate dismissal. Please keep me informed of the status of this action

If you have any questions please feel free to reach me at 212-266-1607. Thank you.

C00622

DW:mpa

pc: Richard B. Shapiro, Assistant Commissioner, Technical Dev.
Andrew Schlein, Acting Executive Director, MIS
File

EXHIBIT 10. *Systems Director recommends dismissing me, dated July 16, 1993.*

CHAPTER TWENTY-TWO

VISITORS PASS OUT OF TITLE ARBITRATION

Ashes, not even identifiable ashes. Dust.
It does not exist. It never existed.
ORWELL.

In March 1991, my supervisor, the Program Manager, instructed me to develop the Visitors Pass system. The system was designed to track and control the flow of visitors in and out of the Department's facilities. This assignment was difficult as the Visitors Pass system was to be written in COBOL-CICS. COBOL is a computer programming language for batch computer processing. But CICS is not a computer programming language. CICS is middleware for online interactive processing. I knew COBOL but I did not know CICS. No one in the Information Systems Division knew any CICS. There was no one to guide me or to whom to ask questions.

The Program Manager knew COBOL but he did not know CICS. He refused to help me or in any way involve himself with the Visitors Pass system. Several months passed and he barely spoke to me. The other computer programmers were sent on Admins training courses but he would not send me on a CICS training course. He told me that I had to learn CICS from a CICS manual. He ordered me - commence coding! In April 1991, the Executive Director called me to his office. He threatened to bring me up on disciplinary charges to terminate my employment if I did not complete the Visitors Pass system. I completed the Visitors Pass system in September 1991. I showed it to a co-worker and he said that it was good.

I approached the Union and I told the Representative that the Visitors Pass system was out of title but she refused to file my grievance. She told me that if a grievance were to be filed, then it would lose. She explained that the management have a right to mismanage and that the Visitors Pass system was not out of title work. There existed the Collective Bargaining Agreement between the City and the Union, but I was not a party to this Agreement. I was an aggrieved employee on my own and I had no standing to invoke the Agreement's out of title grievance procedure.

I was a computer programmer, not a lawyer, nor had I been trained in labor relations law. It seems that a computer programmer job requires the skills of a lawyer. The Union had refused to file my grievance by way of the Collective Bargaining Agreement. How could I grieve the Visitors Pass system as out of title without having the support and approval of the Union? It took me several months to solve this problem.

I reviewed the Department's Rules and Regulations. Fortunately the Department's Rules and Regulations did specifically address out of title work. I discovered that an alternate procedure for filing a grievance did exist and that it was available. I could file my grievance on my own pursuant to the Department's Rules. I succeeded in teaching myself CICS without training, in completing the Visitors Pass assignment without the help of the Program Manager and in grieving the Visitors Pass system without the support of the Union.

To my astonishment, the national office of the Union then stepped forward to take my grievance to binding arbitration, according to the Union-City Collective Bargaining Agreement. According to this Agreement, both parties, Union and City, agreed to be bound by the findings of the Arbitrator. In June 1993, the Arbitrator held a hearing and both parties, Union and City, were legally represented. There were two matters for the Arbitrator to decide. Did I file the grievance on time? Was I was working within title or out of title?

The grievance should properly have been filed within days of the Program Manager giving me the Visitors Pass assignment. I lost several months of compensation because I had not filed my grievance straightaway. I had not filed my grievance straightaway because the Union Representative refused to file the grievance on my behalf and I had no standing to invoke the grievance procedure of the Collective Bargaining Agreement on my own. The Arbitrator wrote that it was "unfortunate that Grievant was not encouraged enough by the comments made by his union representative."

The Arbitrator decided that I did not file my grievance on time and she gave me only a partial award, not a full award. She awarded me the difference between the pay of a Computer Associate and the pay of a Computer Specialist from the day that I filed my out of title grievance to the day that I completed the Visitors Pass system. The Department paid out this award by adding a single payment to my regular bi-monthly salary pay slip. Purely from a cash viewpoint, the Department had done as it had been required to do.

The Arbitrator decided that I had worked out of title on the Visitors Pass system. She decided that I had worked out of title from when the Program Manager gave me the assignment until I completed the assignment. The job specification for a Computer Associate: under direct supervision, carries out technical assignments. For a Computer Specialist: under supervision, carries out highly technical assignments. I persuaded the Arbitrator that my work on the Visitors Pass system was highly technical and that my supervisor did not help me with my work.

I testified to the Arbitrator that the Visitors Pass system was a highly technical assignment which I completed without supervision. I testified that my supervisor, the Program Manager, had assigned the Visitors Pass system to me, that I had completed the system, that work on the system had occupied all of my worktime, that the system was highly technical, that my supervisor did not help me and that the Executive Director had threatened to bring charges and terminate my employment if I did not complete the system. I showed the Arbitrator the memorandum which the Program Manager gave to me which assigned the Visitors Pass system to me. I told the Arbitrator that I requested CICS training, but that my supervisor referred me to the manual. To support my argument that the work was highly technical, I showed the Arbitrator the manual which said that the work was complex but that it could be done by one heroic person.

During my testimony, the Union attorney asked me why I had grieved on my own according to the Department Rules. He asked me why I did not go to the Union so that the Union could file the grievance according to the Collective Bargaining Agreement. I testified that I had been to see the Union Representative but the Representative told me that the Visitors Pass system was not out of title work and that I would lose. I answered the questions put to me by the City's attorney. He showed me memoranda which my supervisor had written to me. I replied that these memoranda did not help me with my work.

The City's witness was a staff analyst from City Personnel Department who testified before the Arbitrator that he had conducted a desk audit. He testified that he had consulted with the Department's Associate Personnel Director of Management Information Systems, and with the managers in the Department of Correction Information Systems Division. The City's witness testified to the Arbitrator that the managers advised him that my work on the Visitors Pass system was not out of title.

In July 1993, the Arbitrator rendered her decision to the New York City Office of Collective Bargaining. The case number is A-4245-92. She found in my favor and she vindicated my grievance. She found that my work on the Visitors Pass system was out of title. In a 13-page decision, the Arbitrator found that, *"From March 11, 1991 through September 20, 1991, Grievant, working alone, developed the Visitors Pass system....the Visitors Pass system was highly technical in nature and had been completed with little supervision...the duties and responsibilities performed by Grievant...were those of Computer Specialist."*

The Arbitrator had rendered a decision that went beyond a simple cash award. She decided that, from March 1991 until September 1991, I had completed the Visitors Pass system, that I had performed the duties of a Computer Specialist and that my work had been out of title. She decided that this was a highly technical assignment and that I had accomplished this all by myself without help from my supervisors.

The Union and the City of New York entered into the Collective Bargaining Agreement by which the decision of the Arbitrator is final and binding. The Arbitrator found that I had completed the Visitors Pass system and that my work had been out of title. I won.

The Commissioner and her Department were bound by the Arbitrator's decision. The managers supervising me were officers of the Department of Correction and so, according to the Collective Bargaining Agreement, they too were bound by the Arbitrator's decision.

The Arbitrator decided that I had completed the Visitors Pass system with little help from my supervisors. But my supervisors gave me performance evaluations which said that I had not completed any assignments.

The managers never gave me the credit which I deserved. The managers should have said thank you when I completed the Visitors Pass system. They should have commended me for a job well done. Instead, they held an office party and everyone was invited - everyone except for me. This was a phantasmagoria. The Visitors Pass system was an incredibly shrinking assignment which vanished into nowhere as if it never existed. It reminds me of "Nineteen Eighty-Four" where O'Brien holds up a photograph to Winston Smith, tosses the photograph into the incinerator and then denies that the photograph ever existed.

No one helped me with the Visitors Pass system. While I was busy developing the Visitors Pass system, the managers were on Mount Olympus hurling charges and thunderbolts at me. After I completed the Visitors Pass system, the Department and its managers insisted that I had not completed any assignment. The managers wrote eight pages of negative performance evaluations which said that I was a troublemaker, I lacked initiative, I had not completed any assignments and my performance had been unacceptable. Yet, in these eight pages, they did not once mention the Visitors Pass system.

The Arbitrator's decision was binding but the Department and its managers refused to acknowledge her decision. The Executive Director gave me a corrective interview calling me unprofessional and disruptive. The Commissioner told the City Council President that my out of title grievance had no merit. The Assistant Commissioner wrote that I was incompetent and that I had done absolutely no work.

The managers mocked and nullified the Arbitrator's decision. The Visitors Pass system was an inconvenient fact which they sought to suppress. It punctured their narrative that I was incompetent and that I had done absolutely no work. They were not going to let the facts get in the way of writing negative performance evaluations and terminating my employment. Had I completed the Visitors Pass system? Yes, said the Arbitrator. No, said the evaluations. Just like the photograph in "Nineteen Eighty-Four", the Visitors Pass system had ceased to exist. It had never existed.

grievance with the Department of Corrections that I am working "Out of Title'" and specifically makes out an out-of-title claim. (Joint Exhibit 1). Unlike his May 9 memorandum to Hickox, Grievant clearly asserts his contractual rights in the September memorandum and states the basis for his claim as "out-of-title." Such a clear and unambiguous letter, which specifically states Grievant's claim and intentions, constitutes the Step I filing of the grievance which gave rise to this matter.

Accordingly, Grievant did not file his Step I grievance within thirty days of the assignment to the work, as he began working on the project March 11 and filed his Step I grievance on September 11. Article VI, Section 2 of the collective bargaining agreement precludes an out-of-title pay award for any period prior to the filing of the Step I grievance, unless the grievance had been filed within thirty days of the assignment. Thus, if Grievant is found to have performed out-of-title work, he will be limited to an award calculated only from the date of his Step I filing on September 11.

With respect to Grievant's out-of-title claim, it was unrebutted that he had been performing duties substantially different from those in the job specifications of a Computer Associate, Level I. Thus, I find that Grievant had been performing out-of-title duties during that time he had been engaged in the design of the Visitors Pass System.

The main distinction between the Computer Associate and Computer Specialist titles, as relevant to this matter and as found in the specifications, is that an Computer Associate may design a computer system or related software function "under direct supervision" with "moderate latitude for independent action . . . or judgment " while a Computer Specialist performs similar duties "under supervision, with considerable latitude for independent action or the exercise of independent judgment."

Grievant's testimony was uncontroverted that his work on the Visitors Pass system was highly technical in nature and had been completed with little supervision and with considerable latitude for independent judgment. The testimony of Desk Auditor Glassberg

EXHIBIT 11. *Arbitrator's decision that I completed out of title Visitors Pass system, dated July 19, 1993.*

AWARD

On the basis of the evidence of record, the grievance is sustained in part and denied in part.

It remained unrebutted that Grievant performed duties from March 11, 1991 to September 20, 1991, which were substantially different from those stated in his job description of Computer Associate. In addition, the duties and responsibilities performed by Grievant during the period in question were those as described in the job specifications of Computer Specialist.

Grievant, however, did not file a Step I grievance with respect to his out-of-title claim until September 11, 1991. Accordingly, Grievant shall receive the difference in pay between a Computer Specialist and a Computer Associate for the period September 11, 1991 through September 20, 1991, pursuant to Article VI, Section 2 of the collective bargaining agreement.

STATE OF NEW YORK)
COUNTY OF BRONX) ss:

I, ROSEMARY TOWNLEY, ESQ., Ph.D., do hereby affirm upon my oath as an ARBITRATOR, that I am the individual described in and who executed this instrument, which is my OPINION AND AWARD.

Dated: July 19, 1993

Rosemary Townley, Esq., Ph.D.

EXHIBIT 11. *Continued.*

CHAPTER TWENTY-THREE

U.S. EQUAL EMPLOYMENT OPPORTUNITIES COMMISSION

There's nothing so lonesome, so morbid or drear
than to stand in a bar, of a pub with no beer.
SLIM DUSTY.

Title VII is the Federal law to address employment discrimination. The law prohibits religious discrimination, harassment and discrimination in the workplace. It requires reasonable accommodation for Sabbath observance. It protects the right of an employee to request reasonable accommodation. The U.S. Equal Employment Opportunity Commission (EEOC) is responsible for investigating complaints and enforcing the law. The EEOC considers it reasonable accommodation to use lunch hours in exchange for early departure and to permit an employee to make up time lost due to the observance of religious practices.

The law requires the employee to exhaust certain administrative procedures before he can bring his complaint to Court. The law requires the employee first to bring his complaint of employment discrimination to the EEOC, within 180 days of the alleged incident of discrimination occurring. The EEOC has 180 days to investigate the complaint. This provides the EEOC with the opportunity to investigate and, perhaps, to mediate a resolution. This could succeed in the best case scenario when the EEOC does actually investigate a complaint. After 180 days have passed, the employee may request a Notice of Right to Sue from the EEOC. The law then allows the employee 90 days, from when the EEOC issues the right-to-sue letter, to bring his complaint to Court.

The law requires the employee to complain to the EEOC, with the hint that the EEOC will somehow afford protection during the course of an investigation ("enforcing Federal laws"..."protected activity"). But the EEOC does not protect those who approach it. The complaint to the EEOC alerts the employer that there is a six-month window of time in which to retaliate against the employee. This six-month window invites retaliation because the employee is helpless while the incorrigible employer retaliates against him and the EEOC does not protect him and he is not yet permitted to bring his Title VII complaint to Court.

Moreover the requirement for the employee to present a right-to-sue letter from the EEOC to the Court creates legal complications concerning of the tolling of the 180 days for the employee to complain to the EEOC, the 180 days for the EEOC to issue the right-to-sue letter and the 90 days for filing the complaint with the Court. The employee has to find an attorney. The attorney has to interview the employee to find out the facts. Then the attorney has to write out the complaint, serve the summonses and file the complaint. 90 days is scarcely enough time to do all of this.

The law requires an employee to be so courageous that he will stick his neck out and complain to the EEOC, knowing full well that his employer might retaliate against him, yet without hope that the EEOC will protect him from the retaliation. For the employee who is fearful of being retaliated against, he might rather remain silent in the face of discrimination until he has found a better job elsewhere, or he might quit. If the EEOC does not investigate a complaint, then the requirement that the employee brings a right-to-sue letter from the EEOC is unlikely to reduce workplace discrimination but it may discourage a timid employee from complaining to the EEOC about discrimination.

On October 8, 1991, I approached the Department of Correction's EEO Officer to request accommodation for Sabbath observance. But the EEO Officer remained silent. Two weeks later, the Department and its managers retaliated against me. On October 23, 1991, they revoked my computer password and they brought me up on disciplinary charges.

In December 1991, I visited the EEOC at its local office in New York City which, at that time, was in the old World Trade Center. I complained that the Department of Correction and its managers did not reasonably accommodate my Sabbath observance. I complained that they revoked my computer password and brought charges against me because I had made the request. In subsequent months I returned to the EEOC and brought additional complaints. I complained to the EEOC that the other computer programmers were sent on training courses while I was left behind. I complained the Systems Director had shouted at me, that he attempted to demote me and that he intended to terminate my employment. I complained of inappropriate work assignments and negative performance evaluations to retaliate against me because I requested accommodation for Sabbath observance.

I brought my complaint to the EEOC but, without my consent, the EEOC outsourced my complaints to the New York State Division of Human Rights (SDHR). The SDHR sent three letters to the Department of Correction but the Department did not respond.

In March 1992, the Department's EEO Director browbeat me to repudiate my complaint but I would not sign her agreement. I wanted the EEOC to investigate my complaint.

In June 1992, the SDHR found probable cause because I had charged the Department with discrimination but the Department did not respond. Probable cause means that, upon the evidence presented, there is sufficient reason to believe that the Department of Correction had discriminated against me. After the SDHR found probable cause, the Department of Correction then applied to the SDHR to vacate its finding of probable cause. The Department argued that it had not responded because it had not received the complaint. Not received the complaint - what?

In February 1993, upon the request of the Department of Correction, the SDHR vacated its probable cause finding and it reopened its investigation. The SDHR declared that the complaint had been sent to the wrong address. Wrong address - what? According to its own records, on three different dates, the SDHR wrote to the Commissioner for Correction at 60 Hudson Street. This is the correct address. Despite the declaration by the SDHR that the complaint had been delivered to the wrong address, I believe that the letters had been delivered to the Commissioner's office. I believe that the Department had indeed received the complaint. I believe that the Department did not respond to the SDHR because the managers chose not to cooperate in the investigation.

According to the Assistant Commissioner's memorandum to the Commissioner, the probable cause finding had been due to the incorrect handling of the complaint by the Department of Correction. So the letters had been received by the Department but the Department had incorrectly handled the complaint. So then, why did the SDHR say that the letters had been sent to the wrong address? And why did the SDHR reward the Department's incorrect handling of the complaint by vacating the probable cause finding? The plot thickens. Why indeed? But there is a simple answer.

From 1986 until 1992, when she became Commissioner for Correction, Catherine Abate had been the Executive Deputy Commissioner for the SDHR. She had influence and connections. She had friends and colleagues in the SDHR and she knew their telephone numbers. I believe that the Commissioner for Correction picked up the phone to call in a favor. I believe that the SDHR vacated its probable cause finding, not because the complaint had been sent to the wrong address, but because Commissioner Catherine Abate placed a phone call to a senior official at the SDHR to request a professional courtesy.

The SDHR vacated its probable cause finding. It reopened its investigation but I told the SDHR that I wanted my complaints to be investigated by the EEOC. Title VII is Federal law and the EEOC is the appropriate Federal authority to handle the investigation. I wanted an impartial investigation to be held by the EEOC.

I first complained to the EEOC in December 1991. By August 1993, no one, not the Department's EEO Director, nor the SDHR nor the EEOC had investigated my complaints. The law only required me to wait for six months, but I gave the EEOC additional time. I waited eighteen months to see whether the EEOC would investigate my complaints. Why did I complain to the EEOC? Was it because I felt miserable and I needed a grief counselor with whom to vent my frustrations? Rather I complained to the EEOC that the Department of Correction and its managers were engaging in employment discrimination. My complaint needed investigation by the Federal agency charged with investigating complaints.

The EEOC did not do its job. It neither began to investigate any of my complaints, nor protected me from harassment. My computer password had been revoked. I had been served charges and given negative performance evaluations. The other computer programmers were sent on training courses while I was left behind and instructed to study the manual. Yet in these eighteen months, the EEOC did not assign an investigator to my case.

In July 1993, the Assistant Commissioner transferred me to Personnel Division. The EEOC did not intervene to protect me from the transfer to Personnel. I had long expected the Assistant Commissioner to transfer me to Rikers Island. The EEOC did not protect me from the transfer to Personnel so I had no confidence that the EEOC would protect me from a transfer to Rikers Island. There was no time to lose. It was now urgent and imperative that I get my complaint out of the hands of the EEOC and into the Courtroom, before the Assistant Commissioner transferred me to Rikers Island.

In August 1993, I approached the EEOC to request a Notice of Right to Sue. The EEOC issued the right-to-sue letter and it closed the case. I had exhausted administrative procedures and the right-to-sue letter permitted me to proceed to Court. In September 1993, I brought my complaints of employment discrimination and civil rights violations to Federal Court.

I believe that the administrative procedures are burdensome to the plaintiff, and that the SDHR, the EEOC and the Notice of Right to Sue should all be abolished. The law should permit an aggrieved employee to bring his complaint of Title VII violations directly to Federal Court without first having to approach the EEOC. Just as a personal injury plaintiff is not required to exhaust administrative procedure, so Title VII should not require the plaintiff to exhaust administrative procedure. The law should give an employment discrimination plaintiff as much time to file a charge with the Court as it gives to personal injury plaintiffs. An EEOC that does not investigate complaints is as pointless as a pub with no beer.

CHAPTER TWENTY-FOUR

TRANSFER TO PERSONNEL DIVISION

During my employ with the Department of Correction, I worked at three different locations. First, from April 1990 until July 1993, I worked at the Information Systems Division in Hudson Street, Manhattan. Second, from July 1993 until January 1995, I worked at the Personnel Division in Broadway, Manhattan. Third, from January 1995 until February 1995, I worked at the Telecommunications Division in Rikers Island.

In July 1993, the Assistant Commissioner transferred me from the Information Systems Division to the Personnel Division. He wrote that this was a relocation, not a transfer. The Information System Division was in the Western Union building in Hudson Street and the Personnel Division was by the Woolworth Building on Broadway. Both buildings were in historic downtown Manhattan. I spent more than a year in Personnel, from July 1993 until January 1995. I was the only computer programmer in the Personnel Division. All of the other computer programmers were in the Information Systems building. They worked on the Inmate Information System. The transfer to Personnel had segregated me from the other computer programmers.

In July 1993, the Assistant Commissioner transferred me to Personnel. The next time I saw him was in July 1995, two years later, when he appeared at the Unemployment Benefits hearing to oppose my claim for unemployment benefits. We did not speak to each other at the hearing.

Now that I was in another building, I never again met my supervisor, Systems Director Waldmann. In July 1993 the Systems Director recommended terminating my employment. From July 1993 until February 1995, when I resigned, neither Systems Director Waldmann nor the Assistant Commissioner ever met with me face to face, not even for one minute. He visited Personnel once while I was there, he saw me, but he did not say hello. In October 1991, the managers had revoked my computer password. They prevented me from performing the duties for which I had been appointed. Instead they gave me sham make-work. Every week while I was in Personnel, the Systems Director would write to remind me that I had not completed my assignment, that what I had written was inaccurate and that my assignment was overdue. Every week, I would write a reply reminding him that I had indeed completed my assignment, that it was indeed accurate and I would offer to send to him a copy of the material which I had previously sent to him.

Whether or not the Assistant Commissioner had my happiness in mind when he transferred me to Personnel, the time that I spent in Personnel was relaxing and comfortable. I enjoyed being in the Personnel Division. I had moved from Washington Heights and I was now living in Stuyvesant Town, in southern Manhattan. My commute home was now only 30 minutes. Every lunch break I would go out and have fun exploring the shops and I would eat a steaming hot fresh slice of pizza in the nearby kosher pizza shop.

I stopped being afraid to come to work. The Personnel Director left me alone. The managers and staff of the Personnel Division treated me civilly and with respect. I chatted and joked about with the correction officers who were stationed at the reception desk. I read the newspaper, just as the Systems Director did. I applied myself to my studies and, in February 1994, I was awarded my Master's degree in Public Administration.

CHAPTER TWENTY-FIVE

I BRING COMPLAINT TO COURT

You can't fight City Hall!

I first complained to the EEOC in December 1991. I would rather the EEOC had quickly investigated my complaints and mediated a resolution. But by July 1993, when the Assistant Commissioner transferred me to Personnel, the EEOC had not begun to investigate any of my complaints, nor had it protected me from the harassment. It had not even assigned an investigator to my case. I lost confidence in the EEOC. I anticipated that the Assistant Commissioner was going to transfer me to Rikers Island. The transfer to Personnel was the starting pistol for a race. There was no time to lose. It was now urgent and imperative that I get my complaint out of the hands of the EEOC and into the Courtroom, before the Assistant Commissioner transferred me to Rikers Island.

In August 1993, I requested the EEOC for a Notice of Right to Sue, which was promptly issued. This allowed me to proceed to Court. In September 1993, I brought my complaint of employment discrimination and civil rights violations to Federal Court. Since the Union was not willing to represent me and since no law firm or public interest firm was willing to represent me and since the EEOC had not even begun to investigate any of my complaints, then I would have to represent myself. This is what lawyers call being a pro se plaintiff. I hired a law firm to write my complaint, to serve the summonses, to write certificates of service and to file my complaint with the Court. I complained to the Court that the Department and its managers had failed to reasonably accommodate my Sabbath observance and that they had harassed me and retaliated against me because of my complaints. On the day that I brought my complaint to Court, I was still a permanent civil servant employed by the Department of Correction.

In September 1993, representing myself, I brought my complaint of employment discrimination and civil rights violations to Federal Court pursuant to Federal laws Title VII and Section 1983 and State Civil Service law and State Human Rights law. Rather than a bench trial, I demanded trial by Jury. The fee for filing the complaint was greater because I had demanded trial by Jury. I named Douglas E. Waldmann, Director for Systems Development, as my supervisor, Raymond Hickox as the Executive Director of Management Information Systems and Catherine Abate as the Commissioner for Correction. I also named the Department of Correction and the City of New York. I did not name the Program Manager, as he had not interfered with my Sabbath observance. Nor did I name the Assistant Commissioner, as he had not yet transferred me to Rikers Island.

I complained to the Court that the Department and its managers did not accommodate my Sabbath observance, they had harassed me and they had retaliated against me. They had intentionally inflicted emotional distress. Their behavior had been outrageous. I asked for awards for compensatory and punitive damages. This was a civil case filed in 1993 in Federal Court, Southern District of New York. The index number for this complaint is 6155.

The managers revoked my computer password and served me with charges because I requested accommodation for Sabbath observance. The EEO Officer and the EEO Director mishandled my complaint. They did not treat me with respect, take my concerns into account or make any serious effort to resolve my complaint. By revoking my password, the managers deliberately prevented me from performing the duties for which I had been appointed. They treated me as a pest and they clearly intended to terminate my employment.

The Department and its managers were determined to terminate my employment. I was determined to resist their efforts to terminate my employment. But the forces were not equally balanced. This was not a fair fight. You can't fight City Hall! The City had platoons of paralegals and lawyers galore. How could one resist the might and resources of the City? I was on my own and I was not allowed to speak with fellow employees. I resisted the management provocations and I held on to my job but my employment was precarious. I had to wait and hope that the Court would soon set a trial date. Otherwise the managers would continue to harass me. I had cried out to the Court for relief. If the Court would not intervene to protect me from the harassment, then eventually the managers would succeed in forcing me to resign. The pivotal question was whether the Court would soon set a trial date. The Court kept its doors locked. It remained silent. It did not set a trial date. This silence emboldened the managers. My complaint festered on the Court docket. There was no protection of the law. I was a goner.

What goes around, comes around. Both the Executive Director and the Systems Director got divorced from their wives while serving me with disciplinary charges and seeking to terminate my employment. The summons server told me that he served my employment discrimination summons upon the Systems Director about one hour after his wife had divorce papers served upon him - two sets of legal papers served upon the Systems Director in one hour! It never rains but it pours. The Systems Director's divorce went to Court. He lost. He appealed the decision. He lost.

CHAPTER TWENTY-SIX

EMPLOYMENT DISCRIMINATION AND CIVIL RIGHTS LAW

Pray for the welfare of the government, without fear of which, people would swallow each other alive.
PIRKEI AVOS.

A public sector employee has both the statutory and constitutional right to approach the EEO Officer to request accommodation for Sabbath observance. The law prohibits the employer from retaliating against the employee for making the request. I brought my action to Federal Court pursuant to Title VII and Section 1983. Title VII is about employment discrimination. Section 1983 is about civil rights. Title VII and Section 1983 overlap. They both provide for Jury trial in Federal Court and for punitive damages. An airplane flies with both engines but it can still fly even if one engine fails. A plaintiff can prosecute employment discrimination and civil rights violations with Title VII and Section 1983 harnessed together. The complaint can still fly even if the Court should dismiss one of the causes of action.

Title VII is Federal law prohibiting employment discrimination. By statute, Title VII provides for compensatory damages, injunctive relief, such as reinstatement, and, by common law, punitive damages. Title VII imposes liability upon employers concerning rights of employees in the workplace. It prohibits an employer from terminating or harassing an employee because of his religion. It requires an employer to reasonably accommodate an employee's religious observance and practice if it can do so without undue hardship. Title VII makes it unlawful for the employer to retaliate against employees for requesting accommodation for a religious practice. It prohibits employers from transferring or relocating employees, or treating them differently from similarly situated employees, from denying training, from writing negative performance evaluations of employees, from subjecting employees to hostile working environment, termination or constructive discharge, if the reason is religion or retaliation.

Section 1983 is Federal law to protect civil rights. It imposes liability upon any person who, under color of state law, deprives a citizen of his rights under the Constitution or Federal law. The New York City Department of Correction and its managers are persons acting under color of New York State Correction law. Section 1983 applies the Bill of Rights to the states and it brings the Constitution into Court. The First Amendment provides for freedom of speech and freedom of religion. This includes observing the Sabbath. ("Sherbert"). The Fourteenth Amendment provides for due process. The law says, a permanent civil servant has a property interest in his employment and he is entitled to a due process hearing prior to discharge. ("Loudermill").

Title VII and Section 1983 both provide for Jury trial. If the Jury finds that the employer has violated the law, then it can award compensatory damages to the employee. I needed compensation for the intentional infliction of emotional distress which caused me to be out sick for three months. Furthermore, if the Jury considers the behavior of the defendants to be outrageous, then it can also award punitive damages.

Title VII and Section 1983 have different filing requirements. Title VII actions must be brought within 90 days of the EEOC issuing the Notice of Right to Sue. When it comes to filing a complaint, Section 1983 is more friendly to plaintiffs than Title VII because Section 1983 does not require the plaintiff to file a complaint with the EEOC and obtain a Notice of Right to Sue. Also Section 1983 has longer time limits than Title VII. The limit for a Section 1983 action varies from state to state. It is the same limit as for personal injuries, two years or more.

There is a legal doctrine known as respondeat superior, also known as the master-servant rule, by which an employer has vicarious liability for employees acting within the scope of their employment. Title VII and Section 1983 have different standards for proving that the employer was liable. In Title VII, the doctrine of respondeat superior applies, that is, the employer is legally responsible for the wrongful acts of the employee. To prove that the Department of Correction was liable, one has to show discriminatory or retaliatory intent by the defendants. One has to show that the Commissioner knew or should have known of the harassment and discrimination and that she took no effectual action to correct the situation. In Section 1983, the doctrine of respondeat superior does not apply. The plaintiff has to prove that the Department has an official policy of discrimination. This could make a Section 1983 action more difficult to prove than a Title VII action. However if a manager can be found liable, then it may not be critical to the case to prove that the Department is also liable. The plaintiff has to prove that he has been deprived of a constitutional right and that this right is substantial enough to warrant the protection of federal law and federal courts.

The Commissioner's letter to the City Council President shows that the Commissioner knew and approved of action taken against me by her managers. Consequently the Commissioner and her Department were legally responsible for the discrimination and retaliation. My visit to the EEO Officer was an exercise of freedom of speech and so it was protected by the First Amendment and by Section 1983. The disciplinary charges were not some harmless and amusing prank of the Executive Director. The charges, brought two weeks after my visit to the EEO Officer, represent the official policy of the Department of Correction and of the City of New York. In bringing the charges, the Department violated my freedom of speech.

Title VII and Section 1983 overlap and they are used together in employment discrimination litigation but the origins and intentions of Title VII and Section 1983 are quite different. The Great Society program was launched by President Lyndon B. Johnson to address health care, education, transportation, poverty, voting, housing and discrimination. As part of the Great Society, Congress enacted the Civil Rights Act of 1964. This outlawed discrimination because of race, color, religion, sex, national origin or retaliation. Title VII is part of the Civil Rights Act of 1964 and it prohibits discrimination in the workplace. It prohibits dismissal or harassment because of an employee's religion. It requires an employer to reasonably accommodate an employee's religious observance and practice if it can do so without undue hardship. Congress enacted the Civil Rights Act of 1991 to amend Title VII. The law addresses burden of proof for disparate impact and mixed motivation. It limits compensatory damages to $300,000 and it provides for Jury trial. Title VII requires the exhaustion of remedies.

During the Reconstruction era, following the Civil War, the states ratified the Fourteenth Amendment, which requires the states to provide due process and equal protection. At the same time, Congress enacted Section 1983, which was initially called the Enforcement Act of 1871, which was to suppress the Ku Klux Klan. Section 1983 is an amazing little law, only one paragraph long, that punches above its weight. For ninety years, the law was untested. The Civil War had been a rebellion by the Confederate states against the Federal government. Section 1983 gave recourse to Federal courts for citizens abused by state officials. But when Reconstruction ended, then so ended access to the Federal courts. Federal Judges would not hear Section 1983 complaints, plaintiffs had to seek state remedy, until the "Monroe v Pape" decision of 1961. The "Monell" decision of 1978 allowed plaintiffs to sue municipalities and government officials. Section 1983 does not require the exhaustion of remedies, except prisoners, so it is easier to file than a Title VII action.

A civil servant has a property interest in his employment. Section 1983 brings the Fourteenth Amendment into court and the Fourteenth Amendment provides for due process and equal protection. The civil servant cannot legally be discharged from his employment without a due process pre-termination hearing. Who would have foreseen that a law originally intended to suppress the Ku Klux Klan would be used by civil servants to prosecute civil rights! Even before the Civil War, due process was already included in the Fifth Amendment to the Constitution. The difference is, the Fifth Amendment is a responsibility of the Federal government and the Fourteenth Amendment is a responsibility of the states.

The right of due process was proclaimed by the Magna Carta in 1215. It establishes the principle that the individual has legal rights which the State must respect, it sets out the rule of law and the procedure to be followed for the administration of justice. But the Magna Carta was not as great as its name would suggest because it provided that debts to Jews did not have to be paid; and so began the expulsion of the Jews from England. Unlike the Magna Carta, the Constitution of the United States is kind to Jews because it provides for freedom of religion and for equal protection before the law.

CHAPTER TWENTY-SEVEN

CORRECTIVE INTERVIEW

In some cases, a simple conference with the employee can lead to improved performance and conduct, thus avoiding the necessity for future disciplinary proceedings...Any formal conference or counseling session is not itself a form of discipline and it should be conducted as a positive, informative and constructive exchange between supervisor and employee, not as a reprimand.

NEW YORK STATE DEPARTMENT OF CIVIL SERVICE. MANUAL OF PROCEDURES IN DISCIPLINARY ACTION.

In March 1994, the Executive Director directed me to appear at a corrective interview; this was my third Executive Director. He had a secretary present as a witness. He reprimanded me and he told me that I was unprofessional and disruptive. The Union Representative refused to accompany me and I had to come alone to the corrective interview.

In April 1991, I made personal use of the computer. There was no Departmental regulation prohibiting personal use of the computer. For six months, the managers acquiesced in silence. There had been no word of warning and no corrective interview. In October 1991, I approached the EEO Officer to request accommodation for Sabbath observance. Two weeks later, the second Executive Director revoked my computer password and served disciplinary charges. The pretext for the charges was that I had made personal use of the computer but the real reason for the charges was that I requested accommodation for Sabbath observance.

In April 1993, two years after I made personal use of the computer, the charges were adjourned contemplating dismissal and the second Executive Director was fired. The managers had attempted disciplinary proceedings to terminate my employment - and they had failed. Now what were they going to do?

The Manual for Disciplinary Action explains that the corrective interview itself is not a form of discipline. Corrective interviews are given as a warning to the employee before disciplinary proceedings. A corrective interview can be a simple conference for a positive, informative and constructive exchange between supervisor and employee. The supervisor must give the employee time to assimilate what he has learned from the interview. If the employee heeds the warning and corrects his errant ways, then the interview has been a success. If the employee does not heed the warning, then he faces future disciplinary proceedings.

The purpose of the corrective interview is to avoid the necessity for future disciplinary proceedings. Done right, first comes the warning, second comes the disciplinary proceedings. But in my case, events occurred in the opposite sequence. The managers had put the cart before the horse. In October 1991, the second Executive Director revoked my computer password and served me with disciplinary charges. Then in March 1994, the third Executive Director gave me the corrective interview. This was odd - first came the disciplinary proceedings, second came the warning. Very strange.

I did not deserve a corrective interview. I had completed the highly technical Visitors Pass system on my own with little supervision. The Executive Director should have commended me for a job well done; instead he called me unprofessional and disruptive.

How did the Executive Director get his job? What had he accomplished and who is he to reprimand me? The Executive Director had never passed a civil service exam. Nor had he ever written a computer program. He was an untenured, provisional at-will employee. I was a tenured civil servant. It is inappropriate for a provisional employee to administer a corrective interview to a permanent civil servant.

The corrective interview caused me discomfort and embarrassment. It was neither positive nor informative nor constructive. I had to stay calm and suffer the humiliation in silence. I could not allow the Executive Director to provoke me. I told him that I was unable to discuss the matter without having an attorney present. I submitted a memorandum stating that I considered the corrective interview to be harassment. So ended the corrective interview. It had only lasted for a few minutes.

The City Corporation Counsel argued that I was sarcastic and that the corrective interview was given in good faith. I say, there was nothing corrective about this corrective interview. It was given after the attempt by the managers to bring disciplinary proceedings against me had already failed. It was given while my complaint of employment discrimination was still pending before the Court. I believe that the real reason why the Executive Director called me into his office for a corrective interview was to discourage me from pursuing my complaint against the Department.

PART FOUR

CONSTRUCTIVE DISCHARGE

CHAPTER TWENTY-EIGHT

WRONGFUL TRANSFER TO RIKERS ISLAND

When I use a word, it means just what I choose it to mean. The question is, which is to be master.
LEWIS CARROLL.

In February 1990, I was appointed from the Civil Service list. In April 1991, I was given a satisfactory performance evaluation and I passed probation. I was now a permanent tenured civil servant in the Information Systems Division at the Department of Correction. In September 1991, I completed the Visitors Pass system. In October 1991, I approached the EEO Officer. Two weeks later, the managers revoked my computer password and they served me with disciplinary charges. In April 1993, the charges were adjourned contemplating dismissal. I emerged unscathed and the managers failed to terminate my employment.

The Department employed me as a computer programmer but the managers had revoked my computer password and so I could not do my job. In May 1992 and in July 1993, the managers wrote negative performance evaluations recommending immediate termination of my employment. In July 1993, the Systems Director recommended to the Assistant Commissioner to terminate my employment. The Assistant Commissioner told the Commissioner that I was incompetent, I did absolutely no work and that he was resuming action against me. Since July 1993, neither the Assistant Commissioner nor the Systems Director had met with me.

In August 1993, the EEOC issued my Notice of Right to Sue and in September 1993, I brought my complaint to Court. In February 1994, I was awarded my Master's degree in Public Administration, but I did not announce this for fear of provoking the managers. Then in March 1994, the Executive Director gave me a corrective interview to tell me that I am unprofessional and disruptive. This was to discourage me from pursuing my complaint against the Department, but the Court had not set a trial date and there was nothing more that I could do.

I came to work on time every day. Unlike the other computer programmers, I was given no training. I had no password so I did no work. After the negative performance evaluation, I stopped attempting the sham make-work of documenting old computer programs. I waited either for the Court to set a trial date or for the managers to terminate my employment.

Perhaps the corrective interview had been an attempt to goad me to resign but I did not resign. The corrective interview was an episode in the three-year campaign of harassment. Now what were the managers going to do? It was not difficult to guess. They were going to transfer me to Rikers Island to force me to resign.

In January 1995, the Department's Personnel Director delivered an envelope to me by hand. The envelope contained two memoranda. The first memorandum was from the Assistant Commissioner. It bore the title "Work Location" and it referred to a Payroll Management system. The second memorandum was from the Systems Director. It bore the title "Department Telephone Directory Project". Both memoranda were dated January 13, 1995.

The Assistant Commissioner took the law into his own hands and he transferred me from the Information Systems Division in Manhattan to the Telecommunications Division at the Telecommunications Building in Rikers Island. He wrote, *"Effective at 9:00 am, Monday January 30, 1995, you are to report to Mr. Saverio Sutera, Director of Telecommunications at that location...This relocation of your workplace is not a transfer."* The Assistant Commissioner had a boating license, so he knew how to muddy the waters. Was he stating a fact or was he offering a legal opinion? The Assistant Commissioner did not have a law degree but he had raised an interesting legal question. What is a transfer?

Civil Service law provides that a civil servant cannot be transferred without his consent. But what is a transfer? The law says, a transfer is a pure question of law requiring statutory interpretation. Whenever there is a change in appointing authority, then there is a transfer. Transfer means the change of a permanent employee from a position under the jurisdiction of one appointing authority to a position under the jurisdiction of another appointing authority. ("Vrooman").

The Information Systems Division, in Manhattan, and the Telecommunications Division, in Rikers Island, these are two distinct and separate divisions of the New York City Department of Correction. Information Systems Division is one appointing authority with its own director with authority to manage the division and to appoint employees. Telecommunications Division is another appointing authority with its own director with authority to manage the division and to appoint employees. The Assistant Commissioner wrote: "You are to report to the Director of Telecommunications Division." According to "Vrooman", this was a change in position to the jurisdiction of another appointing authority and so it was a transfer!

I immediately wrote to the Assistant Commissioner to protest the transfer but he did not reply. The Assistant Commissioner had transferred me from Information System Division to Telecommunications Division without my consent. He took action against me without bringing disciplinary charges, without a hearing and without even meeting with me.

The Assistant Commissioner declared me to be incompetent. He promised the Commissioner that he was resuming action against me and he relocated or transferred me to Telecommunications Division in Rikers Island without a hearing. Civil Service law says that the Department and its managers could not transfer or relocate me from Information Systems Division without my consent, without disciplinary charges and without a hearing. The law says, a tenured employee protected by the full panoply of rights accorded by the Civil Service Law must be given a hearing before termination or any other disciplinary action is taken. ("Soto"). The Assistant Commissioner took action against me without a hearing and he violated my rights and protections under Civil Service law.

The civil servant cannot be transferred from his appointing authority without his consent. He must be given a hearing before disciplinary action is taken. Civil Service law clearly says, no transfer without consent, no action without hearing. The Assistant Commissioner called me incompetent and he took action and transferred me, but without my consent and without a hearing. He violated my protections under Civil Service law. But moreover, there are constitutional issues. The civil servant has a Fourteenth Amendment property interest in his employment from which he cannot be deprived without a due process hearing. ("Loudermill").

I believe, reading together "Vrooman", "Soto" and "Loudermill", a civil servant has a constitutionally protected property interest in his appointment to the original appointing authority. He cannot be deprived of this appointment without a due process hearing. In my case, I had a property interest in my appointment to Information Systems Division. The Assistant Commissioner transferred or relocated me from Information Systems Division to Telecommunications Division. He deprived me of my property interest in my appointment to Information Systems Division, without a due process hearing, contrary to the Fourteenth Amendment.

New York Civil Service law is State law, and it properly belongs in a New York court. A notice of claim must be filed. I brought a Section 1983 action to Federal Court alleging that the managers had deprived me of my Fourteenth Amendment rights. My complaint included a Title VII allegation that the managers had discriminated against me because of my religion. I brought Civil Service law into Federal Court under pendent jurisdiction, piggybacking on my Section 1983 and Title VII complaint, since this was the same body of fact.

There are three overlapping laws which address the wrongful termination of civil service employment; Title VII, Section 1983 and New York Civil Service law. Rock, paper, scissors; there are no silver bullets, there is no single clear and simple way to litigate wrongful termination. Under common law, Civil Service law only provides for equitable relief, backpay and reinstatement. Reinstatement is nice but insufficient. I needed compensation for the intentional infliction of emotional distress which caused me to be out sick for three months. Moreover, the Department and its managers had behaved outrageously. Both Section 1983 and Title VII provide for Jury trial with punitive damages.

I came to Court with two separate theories of wrongful termination. First. I was a permanent tenured civil servant and the managers deprived me of my property interest in my appointment without a due process hearing. Second. The managers constructively discharged me because I requested accommodation for Sabbath observance.

AU 011395

THE CITY OF NEW YORK
DEPARTMENT OF CORRECTION
60 HUDSON STREET
NEW YORK, N.Y. 10013-4393

ANTHONY J. SCHEMBRI
COMMISSIONER

RICHARD B. SHAPIRO
ASSOCIATE COMMISSIONER
TECHNICAL DEVELOPMENT
AND PROJECT MANAGEMENT

TO: Cyril Newman, Information Services Division

FROM: Richard B. Shapiro, Associate Commissioner

RE: **WORK LOCATION**

DATE: January 13, 1995

It is the practice of this office to outpost members of the Information Services Division to work locations other than the Seventh Floor of 60 Hudson Street when the needs of the Department indicate. Members of the staff are routinely assigned to sites where their work is used to facilitate the automation process. This practice puts the ISD personnel in direct contact with the users of their work, and vice-versa, which results in more efficient and more effective work products. Currently members of this Division are assigned to a wide variety of locations, both on Rikers Island and in other sites around the Department.

The work assignments given to you involve the conversion of Payroll Management System COBOL (PMS) data into documentation usable by our systems. This information is used by the Telecommunications Division to fulfill their mandates.

For these reasons, we have determined that your work production would be better served by being performed at the location of the end users, the DOC Telecommunications Division, located at the Telecommunications Building, 14-12 Hazen Street, Rikers Island N.Y., 2nd floor. **Effective at 9:00 a.m., Monday, January 30, 1995, you are to report to Mr. Saverio Sutera, Director of Telecommunications at that location.** Your assignment to that location will be indefinite. The time between now and then is to be used by you to clean up your work area, so that it may be used by other personnel.

This relocation of your workplace is not a transfer. You are still a part of the Information Services Division, and are accountable to us for your work production. Mr. Douglas Waldmann has given you work assignments to complete as noted in the enclosed memorandum, and will provide schedules for deliverable items. Mr. Waldmann will evaluate your performance. The Telecommunications Division will supervise your time records, including all leave requests, etc.

We also feel that this relocation will allow you the opportunity to complete your work in an atmosphere conducive to success, and away from individual situations which may have impeded your work in the past.

C: Gary M. Lanigan, Deputy Commissioner
Andrew Schlein, Executive Director
Douglas Waldmann, Director
Alan Vengersky, Chief of Personnel
Sam Sutera, Director of Telecommunications

EXHIBIT 12. *Assistant Commissioner's memorandum transferring me to Rikers Island, dated January 13, 1995.*

FROM: Douglas E. Waldmann, Director, Systems Development

TO: Steve Newman, Computer Associate Software

DATE: January 13, 1995

SUBJ: Department Telephone Directory Project

This memo is the outline of a Telephone Directory Project which I am assigning to you. It entails developing programs to build and update files containing information for a Department Telephone Directory. The directory which will follow the format of the existing directory, can then be updated and printed as needed.

The following steps are required:

1. Building of a sequential alpha-ordered file of all active ADWs, Captains and civilians. This file will serve as the basis for the directory.

   File layout: Last Name, First Name, Job Telephone Number, Title, SSN, Facility or Unit.

   Source for Data:

   Report "PR11" (listing of active personnel sorted by last name)

   Personnel Division & Telecommunication's Unit

2. Programming:

   Creation of a new Telephone Directory

   Development of a COBOL program that will add, update, delete records form the base telephone file and produce an up to date listing of employees with their job telephone number.

   Creation of a VSAM file keyed by Social Security Number, also containing the Last Name, First Name and Job Telephone Number (This file will be very useful to MIS.).

More detailed specifications will be provided upon request.

cc: Richard Shapiro
Andrew Schlein

EXHIBIT 13. *Department Telephone Directory Project, dated January 13, 1995.*

CHAPTER TWENTY-NINE

MY WEEK AT RIKERS ISLAND

This ain't no country club.
SHERYL CROW.

Rikers Island is a maximum security complex of several jail facilities which is run by the New York City Department of Correction. There are thousands of inmates and thousands of correction officers. The correction officers are nicknamed New York's Boldest. Rikers Island is notorious as a place of beatings and sexual abuse of inmates by correction officers and of inmates held in solitary confinement. It is notorious for inmate attacks on fellow inmates, on correction officers and on civilian employees. Also it is crowded and unsanitary; an incubator for disease.

Rikers Island is an island of 413 acres in the East River between Queens and the Bronx, close to LaGuardia airport. To get to work, I left my apartment in Stuyvesant Town in Manhattan to take the train to Union Square, then another train to Queensboro Plaza in Long Island City where there is a shuttle bus to Rikers Island. The transfer increased my commute from 30 minutes to one hour and 45 minutes. Upon arrival at Rikers Island, I had to be screened by correction officers and then take another bus to the Telecommunications Building. This second bus is operated by the Department of Correction and it circles around Rikers Island. The razor wire fences surrounding the jail facilities sparkled in the sun, like tinsel on a yuletide tree.

The Telecommunications Building is a separate building in the Rikers Island jail complex. I did not have cause either to enter any of the several jail facilities or to meet any inmates. Throughout my week in Rikers Island, I stayed in the Telecommunications Building, except to eat at the jail cafeteria on the first day. All of the other computer programmers worked in Manhattan. When I started work as a computer programmer in the Information Systems Division, I had never expected to set foot in Rikers Island. I felt alarmed to work in a maximum security area.

I worked in Rikers Island for four days, from Monday, January 30, 1995 until Thursday, February 2, 1995. On Monday, my first day in Rikers Island, I reported to the Telecommunications Director in the Telecommunications Building. He introduced me to the timekeeper and to his secretary, who provided me with a pen and paper, but he did not introduce me to anyone else. The Telecommunications Director did not give me any work assignments. He did not instruct me concerning the Payroll Management System or what information the Telecommunications Division needed from the Payroll Management System to fulfill its mandates; nor did he introduce me to anyone with whom to discuss the Payroll Management System. Nor did he instruct me concerning the Telephone Directory.

I had never before met any of the staff in the Telecommunications Building. There were clerical staff and correction officers. There were computer consultants working for a consulting company. But the Telecommunications Building had no computer programmers employed by the Department of Correction.

I was a computer programmer. The Telecommunications Director provided me with a desk but the desk had no telephone and no computer. I asked the Telecommunications Director for access to a computer but no access was provided. Nor did he restore my computer password. The Assistant Commissioner had transferred me to a maximum security area to work on a Payroll Management assignment with no computer password, no computer, no phone, no training and nobody to speak with.

The Rikers Island jail cafeteria had kosher food readily available. On Monday, I ate a hot kosher meal at the jail cafeteria. On Tuesday morning, the Telecommunications Director told me that I was permitted to eat non-kosher food at the Rikers Island jail cafeteria but that I was forbidden to eat kosher food at the jail cafeteria. On Tuesday, I went hungry.

Also on Tuesday, during my lunch break, the secretary called me to a phone. The call came from the Systems Director. The last time he had spoken to me was in July 1993, over a year ago, when he gave me the negative performance evaluation which recommended terminating my employment. Now he telephoned to ask me whether there was anything I needed. I told him that I needed training. He told me that I did not need any training.

While I was at Rikers Island, I sat alone. No one approached me to discuss work. On Wednesday, I introduced myself to the supervisor of the computer consultants to ask about the Payroll Management system. He told me that he was unaware of any Payroll Management system in the Telecommunications Division. He also told me that there had been a Telephone Directory project which he and his team had already completed. That very moment, the Telecommunications Director briskly walked over and interrupted us. He told me that I was not allowed to speak with the consultants.

The lunch break did not give enough time to leave the island and to return to my desk. The Telecommunications Director would not allow me to eat kosher food in the jail cafeteria. On Wednesday, I used my lunch break to stroll on the road outside the Telecommunications building and to think things over. That afternoon the Telecommunications Director told me that I was not allowed to leave the Telecommunications Building during my lunch break as this was a maximum security area. True, so it was. But why was I the only computer programmer from Information Systems Division employed to work in a maximum security area? I believe that the managers transferred me to a maximum security area because I requested accommodation for Sabbath observance.

On Thursday, February 2, 1995, my fourth day at Rikers Island, someone placed a swastika on my desk. I resigned.

Cyril Newman

NEW YORK CITY DEPARTMENT OF CORRECTION

INTRA-DEPARTMENTAL MEMORANDUM

TDS 099-95

TO: Richard Shapiro, Associate Commissioner, Technical Dev.& Project Mgmt.

FROM: Sam Sutera, Director, Telecommunications Division

SUBJECT: Telecommunications Building Work Location - Mr Cyril Newman Status

DATE: February 9, 1995

As Per your letter of January 13, 1995, to Mr Cyril Newman, he reported to work on Monday January 30, 1995. Mrs Agatha Michael brought him to my office. I showed him the work area that he would be using. Although he did not have a telephone at his desk, I showed him the two telephones he would be able to receive and make calls from.

Mr Newman advised me that he normally worked the hours from 8:00 a.m. to 4:00 p.m. I said I would check with Mr Waldman his immediate Supervisor/ Assoc. Commissioner R. Shapiro because the memo I received said he was to report at 9:00 a.m. Richard Shapiro said that 8:00 a.m. to 4:00 p.m. was fine. I introduced him to the staff that was present at the time Mrs. Michael, Capt.V. Golden, and Ms. V. Freeman (timekeeper). We walked through the building, pointing out various offices, Bathrooms, Lunchrooms and Facilities. I asked if he brought his lunch or if he would need to buy lunch. He said he had brought his lunch. I explained that he might ask one of the Correction Officers to pick something up for him if they were working off Island and that there was also a lunch wagon that came in the morning and before lunch.

I pointed out to him that for security reasons the PBX Equipment Area was off limits to him and that also for security reasons SOD did not permit people to walk on the Island (i.e. Control Building to the Telecom Building).

EXHIBIT 14. *Telecommunications Director's Memorandum, dated February 9, 1995.*

Mrs Michael provided him with the telephone numbers he might need in the event he was unable to report to work. (718) 546-1018, 1010, 1025, 1014 and the sick desk number that could be used after work hours 718-546-1029.

I confirmed that he had his work assignment from Mr Douglas Waldman. Telecommunications would manage His timekeeping and leave requests. I asked that he check with myself or Agatha Michael, the timekeeper V. Freeman or Captain Golden if he needed any assistance. Mrs Michael worked out a lunch and break schedule which he selected 10 a.m., 12 noon and 2:30 p.m.

He said he required a terminal with access to Citynet. I passed his request onto Mr Waldman. Pens, pencils and paper were supplied by Mrs Michael.

At 3.55 p.m. I stopped by his desk to see if he was settled in, in his new work space and I was informed by the switchboard supervisor, Mrs Betty Meeks that Mr Newman left at 3:40 p.m. His time sheet showed him signing out at 4:00 p.m..

On Tuesday January 31, 1995, Mr Newman arrived before 8:00 a.m.. Later that morning I spoke to Mr Newman regarding his early departure Monday. He said he left to catch the 3:45 p.m. Route bus to the control room. I explained 8:00 a.m. to 4:00 p.m. work schedule meant working until 4:00 p.m. He said he understood and he made a mistake.

He asked Mrs Michael about eating lunch at O.B.C.C. and she gave him a copy of Operations Order 14/88 Re: Partaking of meals. Before lunch time Ms. Annie Freeman called me and said she found a Kosher meal at NIC and could Mr. Newman go there to have lunch? I reminded Ms. Annie Freeman that I could not authorize him to go to NIC. Mrs Michael had told him Operations Order 14/88 did not approve him to go there. It seems he did obtain a Kosher Meal at NIC.

I approved and signed a vacation request for Friday 2/3/95

Wednesday 2/1/95. Mr Newman asked me about having Kosher Meals at O.B.C.C.. I spoke D/W Moore at OBCC Re: Kosher Meals availability and he explained that only Inmates receive them when they are authorized. Although His own Corrections Officers eat at the facility, they could not order a Kosher Meal. It might be given out to eat if an inmate meal was unused, but it could not be ordered for them. I then spoke to Assoc. Commissioner Richard Shapiro Re: this subject and he checked with O.L.R. Asst. Commissioner Richard Yates and I was advised that Operations Order 14/88 does no apply to Civilian Personnel, it applies only to Correction Officers. I informed Mr Newman, G. Armstrong, Valerie Freeman, Annie Freeman, and Agatha Michael. (all civilians present in telecom at the time) of this information.

Mr Newman requested to meet with me with Annie Freeman present. Mr Newman asked why I was barring him to eat at OBCC. I repeated what I told him earlier regarding Kosher meals and also what Associate Commissioner R. Shapiro told me. He then said could he have

EXHIBIT 14. *Continued.*

a Non Kosher meal at OBCC, I said I would have to inquire further however, I was not monitoring Mr Newman's whereabouts at lunch time.

At 2.50 p.m. I saw Mr Newman in the PBX Control Room questioning Mr Tim Farler of Harris Corp. preventing him from doing his work. I called Mr Newman aside and reminded him of my instructions that the PBX area was off-limits and he was not permitted in the area. He said he needed to talk to Harris Corp. since he was doing Telecommunications work. I corrected and reminded him that he did not report to me or Telecommunications. His Supervisor is Mr Doug Waldman and his work assignment was not Telecom and its Vendors.

Thursday 2/2/95 - Had no questions or interaction with Mr Newman.

Friday 2/3/95 Mr Newman took an approved vacation day.

Monday 2/6/95 through Wednesday 2/8/95 Mr Newman was A.W.O.L.

Thursday 2/9/95 advised that Mr Cyril Newman has resigned.

cc: Bert Schell, Legal Dept

EXHIBIT 14. *Continued.*

CHAPTER THIRTY

I RESIGNED FROM MY EMPLOYMENT WITH THE DEPARTMENT

I weep for you, the Walrus said, I deeply sympathize.
LEWIS CARROLL.

In January 1995, the managers transferred me to Rikers Island. I was in Rikers Island for just four days, from Monday, January 30, 1995 until Thursday, February 2, 1995. Then I resigned. I sent a certified delivery letter of resignation to the Personnel Director. The letter stated that conditions at Rikers Island had been horrendous, there was antisemitism and I felt forced to resign.

In October 1991, I approached the EEO Officer to request accommodation for Sabbath observance. Two weeks later, the Department and its managers revoked my computer password and they served me with disciplinary charges. I was out sick for three months because I was so upset. In December 1991, I complained to the EEOC that the Department retaliated against me because I requested accommodation for Sabbath observance. The managers intended to terminate my employment. But the EEOC did not investigate my complaints or protect me from the harassment. In August 1993, upon my request, the EEOC issued a Notice of Right to Sue.

In September 1993, I complained to the Court that the Department and its managers had not reasonably accommodated my Sabbath observance but that they had harassed me and retaliated against me because of my complaints. The Court failed me. It kept its doors locked, it failed to protect me, it remained silent and it did not set a trial date. The silence of the Court emboldened the managers and they learned that they could bait me without consequence. The Department and its managers repeatedly broke the law and violated my rights. The law could not protect me from the harassment because the Court did not enforce the law. I was defenseless. The Court remained silent even as the Department and its managers transferred me to Rikers Island. There was nowhere else left to grieve or complain.

In January 1995, the Assistant Commissioner took the law into his own hands. He transferred me to the Telecommunications Division in Rikers Island. He transferred me without first obtaining my consent or serving charges of incompetency or convening a disciplinary hearing. He violated my rights under Civil Service law and the Fourteenth Amendment. This was the culmination of the three-year campaign of harassment.

This transfer was not an accident. There are no magic typewriters and the memorandum did not write itself. The Assistant Commissioner told his secretary to prepare this memorandum for his signature. The Personnel Director delivered it to me by hand. The order by the Assistant Commissioner for me to report to the Director of Telecommunications on Rikers Island was deliberate and intentional. The Commissioner knew and approved of actions taken against me by the Assistant Commissioner. I had long expected to be transferred to Rikers Island. I wrote to the Assistant Commissioner to protest the transfer but he did not reply.

The Department and its managers segregated me from the other computer programmers in the Information Systems Division and they placed me in a maximum security area, which alarmed me. All of the other computer programmers in the Information Systems Division worked in Manhattan. They had telephones and computers at their desks, they were sent on training courses, and they worked together as a team on the Inmate Information System. I was the only computer programmer who had been transferred to Rikers Island. The Systems Director denied my requests for training.

Instead of reporting to work at Rikers Island, could I perhaps have stayed at home and not resigned? No, that is just what the managers wanted me to do. Then the Department would have fired me for being absent without leave. This would have given the Good People a field day. They would have played devil's advocate and explained to me that I deserved to be fired for absenteeism. I was not sick and so I could not go out on disability. If I failed to report for work at Rikers Island, then the Department would have good cause to terminate my employment.

When I arrived at Rikers Island, the Telecommunications Director did not introduce me to anyone with whom I could discuss work. He told me that I was not allowed to speak with the consultants. My desk had neither a telephone nor a computer. The managers had long ago revoked my computer password and the Telecommunications Director did not provide me with a computer. The computer is a critical tool of the computer programmer's job. To program a computer, one needs to have access to a computer.

The transfer lengthened my commute time and hindered my Sabbath observance. The Telecommunications Director forbade me kosher food at the jail cafeteria, even though there was kosher food available to the other employees and to the inmates. On Thursday, my fourth day at Rikers Island, someone placed a swastika upon my desk.

The swastika is the emblem of antisemitism. I resigned straight after I found the swastika. The time had come. It was now appropriate and reasonable for me to resign. Enough is enough. I could not bear to stay one more day in the Department. There was no choice but to resign, claim unemployment benefits and look for another job.

From October 1991, when I requested accommodation for Sabbath observance, until February 1995, when I resigned, the managers harassed me and harassed me, again and again. The Good People told me that I should have complained about the swastika and that I had made a mistake to resign. Now that I had resigned, they told me to get a job, any job, because anything is better than nothing.

The courts discourage employees from resigning. The law says, society and the policies underlying Title VII will be best served if, wherever possible, unlawful discrimination is attacked within the context of existing employment relationships. ("Bourque"). The managers retaliated against me because I requested accommodation for Sabbath observance. For three years, from October 1991 to February 1995, I had been persona non grata. I held out for as long as I could. I clung to my job as tenaciously as a clam clings to a rock. The managers took a hammer and chisel against me. Strike after strike, they pried me loose from the job. But the EEOC did not investigate my complaint and the Court remained silent and it did not set a trial date. Unlawful discrimination was not being attacked from within the context of my existing employment relationship with the Department of Correction.

Could I complain about the swastika? For over three years I had been complaining, but no one paid attention to my complaints. I had given ample notice of employment discrimination to the Department. Not only did the Department and its managers not listen to my complaints but they retaliated against me for my complaints. Neither the Collective Bargaining Agreement nor the Department Rules included any procedure that provided for grieving the swastika. I complained to the Union, the EEO Officer and EEO Director, the Inspector General, the Assistant Commissioner, the Personnel Director, the City Labor Relations Director, the Commissioner for Correction, the EEOC and to the Federal Court. They heard my cries for help and they failed to protect me from the harassment.

It was not easy for me to leave a job that I had fought so long and hard to preserve. The managers succeeded in causing me to resign, but not because I had made a mistake and not because the Assistant Commissioner had outwitted me. My complaint lay before the Federal Court. The Court failed to protect me and it did not set a trial date. There was nowhere else left to grieve or complain. There was no relief, protection or escape from the harassment. I could not bear to stay one more day in the Department. I resigned. I quit. I threw in the towel.

Before the transfer to Rikers Island, I had to do whatever was necessary and reasonable in order to remain employed. I was determined to remain on the job to earn a livelihood and to serve my employer. The Department continued to pay my salary and I continued to come to work every day. But the transfer to Rikers Island aggravated the situation. This was not a voluntary resignation - the Assistant Commissioner had me in checkmate.

CHAPTER THIRTY-ONE

LETTER OF RESIGNATION

I have never been a quitter.
RICHARD NIXON.

On October 8, 1991, I approached the Department's EEO Officer to request accommodation for Sabbath observance. Two weeks later, on October 23, 1991, the Department and its managers revoked my computer password and served me with disciplinary charges. In December 1991, I complained to the EEOC that the Department had harassed me and retaliated against me because I requested accommodation for Sabbath observance. In May 1992 and in July 1993, the managers gave me performance evaluations stating that they intended to terminate my employment.

In May 1992, upon taking office, the Commissioner published a statement saying that she expected vigorous efforts to create a workplace environment where everybody is treated with dignity. In June 1993, the Systems Director shouted at me. I complained to the Commissioner and she remained silent. The Department did not have an effective policy for reporting and resolving complaints.

The Assistant Commissioner wrote to the Commissioner saying that I am incompetent and he is resuming action against me. In January 1995, the Assistant Commissioner transferred me to work in the Telecommunications Building at the Rikers Island jail complex. I immediately wrote to the Assistant Commissioner to protest the transfer but he did not reply. Nor did he meet with me. I was in Rikers Island from Monday, January 30, 1995 until Thursday, February 2, 1995.

The transfer to Rikers Island increased my commute home from 30 minutes to one hour and 45 minutes. In his memorandum transferring me to Rikers Island, the Assistant Commissioner remained silent as to how the Department would accommodate my Sabbath observance. The Telecommunications Director did not explain how he intended to accommodate my Sabbath observance. I felt alarmed to work in a maximum security area. I had no computer password. Despite my request, he did not provide access to a computer. He told me that I was not allowed to eat kosher food at the jail cafeteria.

On Thursday, February 2, 1995, someone placed a swastika upon my desk. On Friday, I did not go into work. On Monday, February 6, 1995, I wrote a certified delivery letter of resignation to the Personnel Director complaining of antisemitism. The Post Office delivered to me a signed certified mail return receipt card, dated February 13, 1995. There was no reply.

The following week, on Thursday, February 9, 1995, I visited the Personnel Division to hand in my identity card and my copy of the Department's Rules and Regulations. I submitted a handwritten version of my letter of resignation on an official Departmental resignation form. An employee gave me a signed receipt. There were now two identically worded letters of resignation. One letter was printed, this I mailed certified delivery. One was hand-written, this I delivered by hand. Both letters said that I had resigned because of antisemitism. There was no reply.

Could it be that the Department had not received the letter of resignation? The Assistant Commissioner said that the letter had not been received. The Unemployment Benefits Judge decided that the letter had not been received. But the Unemployment Benefits Appeal Board reversed the judge's decision. The law says, the petitioner's claim that he never received the notice is insufficient to rebut the presumption of receipt created by the signed certified mail return receipt card. ("Fodor"). So it is presumed that the Department had received my letter. I had a signed certified mail return receipt card from the Post Office dated February 13, 1995 and I had a signed receipt written by the Personnel employee dated February 9, 1995. Two signed dated receipts! It is compelling that the Department and its managers had received the letters of resignation. There was no reply.

When an employee resigns, then the Department provides him with a Letter of Recommendation. The Department of Investigation confronted the Program Manager about his residential address. He resigned and the Department provided him with a recommendation. But when I resigned, the Department did not provide me with a letter. I believe the reason why the Department did not provide me with a letter of recommendation is that I had filed a complaint with the EEOC. The law says that refusal to provide employment references in retaliation for filing a complaint with the EEOC could amount to a violation of Title VII. ("Pantchenko").

The last time any manager of the Department spoke to me was when the Telecommunications Director told me that I was not allowed to speak with the consultants. I had served the Department for over four years and I had completed the Visitors Pass system. There was never a word of gratitude. I resigned after four years of service. The Department should have written a letter of recommendation to thank me for my service and to wish me success in my career. There was no valedictory dinner for me and there was no golden parachute. There was a swastika on my desk and I resigned.

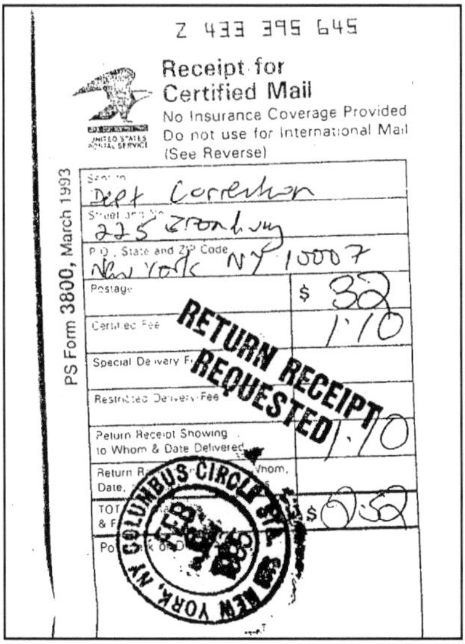

Z 433 395 645

Receipt for Certified Mail
No Insurance Coverage Provided
Do not use for International Mail
(See Reverse)

PS Form 3800, March 1993

Sent to Dept Correction	
Street and No. 225 Broadway	
P.O., State and ZIP Code New York NY 10007	
Postage	$ .32
Certified Fee	1.10
Special Delivery Fee	
Restricted Delivery Fee	
Return Receipt Showing to Whom & Date Delivered	1.10
Return Receipt Showing to Whom, Date, and Addressee's Address	
TOTAL Postage & Fees	$ 2.52
Postmark or Date	

RETURN RECEIPT REQUESTED

COLUMBUS CIRCLE STA. NEW YORK, NY FEB 1995

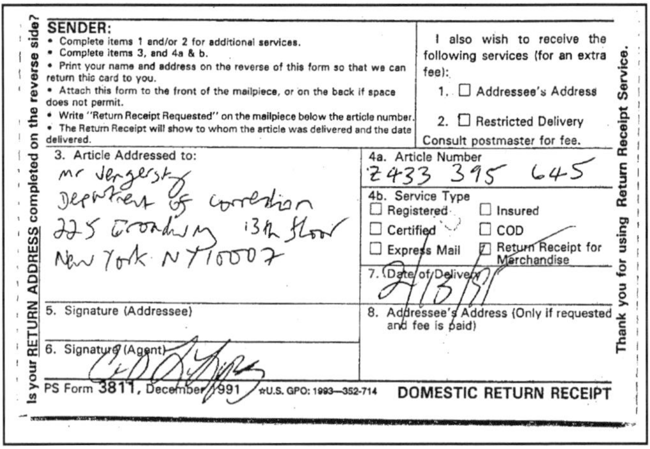

Is your RETURN ADDRESS completed on the reverse side?

SENDER:
- Complete items 1 and/or 2 for additional services.
- Complete items 3, and 4a & b.
- Print your name and address on the reverse of this form so that we can return this card to you.
- Attach this form to the front of the mailpiece, or on the back if space does not permit.
- Write "Return Receipt Requested" on the mailpiece below the article number.
- The Return Receipt will show to whom the article was delivered and the date delivered.

I also wish to receive the following services (for an extra fee):
1. ☐ Addressee's Address
2. ☐ Restricted Delivery

Consult postmaster for fee.

3. Article Addressed to:
Mr Vergesty
Department of Correction
225 Broadway 13th floor
New York NY 10007

4a. Article Number
Z 433 395 645

4b. Service Type
☐ Registered ☐ Insured
☐ Certified ☐ COD
☐ Express Mail ☑ Return Receipt for Merchandise

7. Date of Delivery
2/13/95

5. Signature (Addressee)

8. Addressee's Address (Only if requested and fee is paid)

6. Signature (Agent)

PS Form 3811, December 1991 ☆U.S. GPO: 1993—352-714 DOMESTIC RETURN RECEIPT

Thank you for using Return Receipt Service.

EXHIBIT 15. *USPS certification that Department received letter of resignation, dated February 13, 1995.*

CHAPTER THIRTY-TWO

THE DEPARTMENT AND ITS MANAGERS INTENDED TO TERMINATE MY EMPLOYMENT

If you can keep your head when all about you
are losing theirs and blaming it on you.
KIPLING.

I passed the Civil Service examination for Computer Associate Software. I was selected from the list and appointed to the Information Systems Division of the New York City Department of Correction. I served a year of probation and the Program Manager gave me a satisfactory performance evaluation. In April 1991, I became a permanent tenured civil servant.

In March 1991, Raymond Hickcox was appointed Executive Director. He replaced Bob Creed. In April 1991, Executive Director Hickox called me into his office and told me that I am obnoxious. He canceled the accommodation for Sabbath observance that Bob Creed had approved. He threatened to bring me up on charges and dismiss me from my employment if I did not complete the Visitors Pass system. I completed the Visitors Pass system in September 1991. The Arbitrator decided this was a highly technical assignment, which I had completed with little supervision, and that I was entitled to an award for out of title work.

In October 1991, the clocks were set for daylight

savings. I approached the Department's EEO Officer to request accommodation for Sabbath observance. Two weeks after I met with the EEO Officer, Executive Director Hickox revoked my computer password and served me with disciplinary charges of misconduct. In August 1992, the Program Manager resigned. In April 1993, the charges were adjourned contemplating dismissal and Executive Director Hickox was dismissed. But the managers did not restore my computer password and they still intended to terminate my employment.

Should I have complained? I complained to the Union, the EEO Officer and EEO Director, the Inspector General, the Assistant Commissioner, the Personnel Director, the City Labor Relations Director, the Commissioner for Correction, the EEOC and to the Federal Court. I complained that the managers did not accommodate my Sabbath observance, they discriminated against me because of my religion and they harassed me. I complained that, because I approached the EEO Officer, the managers retaliated against me by revoking my computer password and serving me with disciplinary charges.

The harassment continued for three years. I complained and nobody listened. The more I complained, the more the managers harassed me. The EEOC did not investigate my complaint or protect me from the harassment. The Court remained silent and it did not set a trial date.

In May 1992, the Program Manager gave me a negative performance evaluation and recommended terminating my employment. A few days later, he told me that I was a dead man. In June 1993, Systems Director Waldmann shouted at me that I am incompetent and crazy. In July 1993, he gave me a negative performance evaluation and recommended terminating my employment.

There were three ways by which the managers could terminate my employment: letter of termination, removal by civil service disciplinary hearing or constructive discharge.

The managers wanted to fire me on the spot or give me two weeks' notice and a letter of termination. But the open and straightforward dismissal of a tenured civil servant without any hearing would be a flagrant violation of the law.

Civil Service law provides for removing tenured civil servants for misconduct or incompetency. In New York City, civil service disciplinary hearings are held by the Office of Administrative Trials and Hearings ("OATH"). If the managers were not satisfied with my work performance, then they should have charged me with incompetency and given me a hearing before an OATH Judge.

Why did they stop short? What held them back? The managers doubted whether they could persuade an OATH Judge that I was incompetent. They remembered that, in October 1991, they had served me with disciplinary charges, and they had failed to prove their case. They ended up with egg on their face. They did not dare bring me up on charges a second time. By forcing me to resign, the Department and its managers avoided their constitutional obligation to provide me with my due process right to a hearing and with the opportunity to tell my side of the story.

The managers made a renewed and determined effort to terminate my employment once and for all; but to dismiss me in a manner that was sly, oblique and indirect. In January 1995, the Assistant Commissioner had a memorandum hand-delivered to me. He transferred me to Rikers Island to report to the Director of Telecommunications Division. No other computer programmer had ever been relocated to Rikers Island.

This was not an open and straightforward termination of employment. The transfer was a dismissal that did not call itself a dismissal. It was a termination of employment by other means.

Civil Service law says that the managers could not transfer me without my consent, nor could they take action against me without a hearing. But the intrepid Assistant Commissioner circumvented the law by calling the transfer a relocation. His memorandum was a carefully camouflaged letter of dismissal. Its real meaning was, by hook or by crook, you are fired! I wrote to the Assistant Commissioner to protest the relocation but he did not reply. He transferred me without meeting with me, without my consent and without a hearing. He pushed me across the board like a chess piece made of wood.

In his memorandum, the Assistant Commissioner wrote that he felt that the atmosphere at Rikers Island would be conducive to success; but he did not explain what there is about the atmosphere of a maximum security jail complex that is conducive to success. He was not being straight with me and he was not concerned with my success.

On the contrary, far from providing an "atmosphere conducive to success," the Assistant Commissioner intended to force me to resign. He told the Commissioner that "actions are resuming against him now." He transferred me to Rikers Island intending to create a work atmosphere so intolerable that I was forced into an involuntary resignation. The law says, if the employer deliberately makes an employee's working conditions so intolerable that the employee is forced into an involuntary resignation, then the employer has encompassed a constructive discharge. ("Young").

The proffered reason for the relocation was to work on the Payroll Management System. But Payroll Management is handled by Personnel Division in Manhattan, not by Telecommunications Division in Rikers Island. The Assistant Commissioner wrote that Telecommunications Division uses information from the Payroll Management System to fulfill their mandates. When I arrived at Rikers Island, the Telecommunications Director did not tell me what information his Division needed to fulfill their mandates. He told me that I was not doing work for Telecommunication Division. So then, why had the managers relocated me to Rikers Island?

Systems Director Waldmann wrote to the Assistant Commissioner, "I am strongly recommending Mr. Newman's immediate dismissal." The Assistant Commissioner wrote to Commissioner Abate, "I concur with Mr. Waldmann's characterization of Mr. Newman as incompetent ....actions are resuming against him now." The managers clearly intended to terminate my employment and they transferred me to Rikers Island to force me to resign.

Commissioner Abate wrote to the City Council President, "The Department is making every effort to resolve the issues." The Commissioner knew and approved of actions taken against me by her managers.

CHAPTER THIRTY-THREE

I HAD EXHAUSTED PROCEDURES AND REMEDIES

Two weeks after I approached the EEO Officer, the managers revoked my computer password and they served disciplinary charges upon me. In December, 1991, I complained to the EEOC. There was a three-year campaign of harassment and discrimination. My computer password was never restored. While the other computer programmers were sent on training classes, I was left behind and told to study the manual. The managers gave me negative performance evaluations which said that I had not completed any assignments and which did not mention that I had completed the Visitors Pass system.

In December 1991, I complained to the City Personnel Director and to the EEOC. In May 1992, I complained to the City Council President. I complained that the managers had revoked my computer password. The City Personnel Director and the City Council President relayed my complaints to the Commissioner, and they wrote that my allegations were serious. The Commissioner replied that the Department takes all complaints of employment discrimination very seriously and it is "making every effort to resolve the issues." But she did not order her managers to restore my computer password.

One has to complain to the employer, otherwise the employer can use failure to complain as an affirmative defense. The law says, an employer may defend itself by showing that it had a readily accessible and effective policy for reporting and resolving complaints which the plaintiff unreasonably failed to use. ("Suders"). But once the employer has been informed, then the employer should take corrective action. What if the harassment persists after the employee has already complained; the employer knows of the complaint but chooses not to take corrective action? I had made my complaint to the EEO Officer, to the EEO Director, to the Commissioner and to the EEOC. Any additional complaint was futile and redundant.

Over three years had passed. I had to come into work every day without a password. I was a computer programmer but I did not have a valid computer password and so I was unable to do my job. The harassment had gone on for too long and I had lost hope of my complaints being investigated. I had been complaining since 1991 to no avail. I had given ample notice of employment discrimination to the Department. I had to live through over three years of harassment and discrimination, all on my own.

I complained to the Union but the Union refused to help me. I complained to the Department's EEO Officer and EEO Director. I complained to the Inspector General. I complained to the Assistant Commissioner. I complained to the Department's Personnel Director. I complained to the City Labor Relations Director. I complained to the Commissioner, I complained to the EEOC and I complained to the Court. The harassment and discrimination continued unabated. I complained of the harassment and discrimination and then the managers harassed and retaliated against me some more because of my complaints of harassment and discrimination.

According to the EEO Director, the Department's policy allows two months to investigate a complaint.

The harassment and discrimination continued for over three years until I resigned. I had complained to the EEOC. I had met my obligation to report my complaint and I had exhausted administrative procedures and remedies. The Department had notice. My complaints of harassment and discrimination fell on deaf ears. The retaliation discouraged me from returning to the EEO Officer to complain about the swastika.

In July 1993, the Systems Director recommended termination of my employment. The Assistant Commissioner told the Commissioner that I was incompetent, that I had done absolutely no work and that he was resuming action against me. The Commissioner knew and approved that the Assistant Commissioner was taking action against me.

In August 1993, after eighteen months, upon my request, the EEOC issued me with a Notice of Right to Sue and it closed the case. Because the case was closed, I could not now return to the EEOC to complain about the swastika. The right-to-sue letter is legal proof that I have exhausted administrative procedures and remedies. Should I have complained about the swastika? To whom could I complain?

Should I have complained about the swastika to the EEO Officer? In October 1991, I approached the EEO Officer to request accommodation for Sabbath observance. Two weeks later, the managers revoked my computer password and served me with disciplinary charges. This retaliation discouraged me from returning to the EEO Officer to complain about the swastika.

In September 1993, I complained to the Court but the Court remained silent. It did not set a trial date and it did not protect me from harassment. I resigned. Should I have complained about the swastika? To whom could I complain?

In January 1995, the Assistant Commissioner transferred me to Rikers Island. He wrote that this relocation will allow me the opportunity to complete my work in an atmosphere conducive to success. He relocated or transferred me to Rikers Island without meeting with me, without my consent and without a hearing. No other computer programmers had ever been transferred or relocated to Rikers Island. I wrote to the Assistant Commissioner and I protested his decision to transfer me to Rikers Island but he did not reply.

On Thursday, February 2, 1995, my fourth day at Rikers Island, someone placed a swastika upon my desk. I resigned. Should I perhaps have complained about the swastika? To whom could I complain? In my letter of resignation, I complained to the Personnel Director about antisemitism, but he did not reply.

It was Groundhog Day, all over again! I had to do whatever was necessary and reasonable in order to remain employed. The complaints had not been resolved and I had brought my complaint to Federal Court. Every day I came in to work expecting to be harassed. There was no protection, relief or escape from the harassment.

Within a week of my arrival at Rikers Island, they hindered my Sabbath observance, they denied me kosher food in the jail cafeteria and someone had placed a swastika upon my desk. I tried to remain on the job. I complained of discrimination but my complaints fell on deaf ears. I had exhausted procedures and remedies. Neither the EEOC nor the Court protected me from the harassment and discrimination. It took the managers three years but finally they succeeded in forcing me to resign.

The Commissioner knew and approved of the actions taken against me. The Court knew of my complaints but it remained silent and it did not protect me from harassment or set a trial date. Should I have complained about the swastika? To whom could I complain? Enough already!

CHAPTER THIRTY-FOUR

UNBEARABLE WORKING CONDITIONS

It's my party and I'll cry if I want to.
You would cry too if it happened to you.
LESLIE GORE.

The Arbitrator decided that, without help from my supervisor, I had completed the highly technical Visitors Pass system. The managers intended to fire me and they called me obnoxious, a troublemaker, a dead man, incompetent, crazy, unprofessional and disruptive. Working for these managers was a degrading, humiliating and debilitating experience.

The Department employed me as a computer programmer. In October 1991, the clocks were set for daylight savings and I approached the EEO Officer to request accommodation for Sabbath observance. Two weeks later the managers revoked my computer password and served me disciplinary charges. The charges were adjourned contemplating dismissal but my computer password was never restored. Because my password had been revoked, I could not do my job. A computer programmer without a computer is like a bus driver without a bus.

When the other computer programs were sent to training classes, I was told to study the manual. When the Information Systems Division held an office party,

I was not invited. I was told not to speak to the other employees and they were told not to speak with me. None of the other computer programmers were ever transferred to Rikers Island.

Systems Director Waldmann instructed me to document old obsolete computer programs. This was sham make-work. There was no business purpose to this documentation. It was work for work's sake. Each time I submitted the documentation, he told me that it was not satisfactory and to do it again. In my performance evaluation, he recommended immediate termination of employment. He wanted me to resign. He provoked me to resign.

The harassment continued for three years, from October 1991 until February 1995. I complained and nobody listened. Commissioner Abate told the City Council President that the Department took complaints of employment discrimination very seriously, and it was making every effort to resolve the issues; but the harassment and discrimination continued unabated. The more I complained, the more the managers harassed me. I complained to the EEOC and to the Federal Court. They heard my cries for help and they failed to protect me from the harassment. The EEOC did not investigate my complaint. The Court remained silent and did not set a trial date.

The status of the work environment is like a traffic light. Green = unremarkable, Amber = hostile work environment, Red = intolerable working conditions. For three years, I had to endure a hostile work environment; but the harassment, discrimination and retaliation did not yet reach the threshold of unbearable working conditions and so I remained in my job and did not resign.

In January 1995, the Assistant Commissioner transferred me to Rikers Island. He wrote to me saying that this was a relocation, not a transfer, and he felt it would be conducive to success. But he also wrote to Commissioner Abate saying that he was resuming actions against me and he transferred me to Rikers Island without my consent, without a hearing and without meeting with me.

This transfer was the culmination of a three-year campaign of harassment, discrimination and retaliation. It was a tangible and adverse employer-sanctioned action which aggravated the situation. The Department and its managers transferred me to Rikers Island to make my working conditions so intolerable as to force me into an involuntary resignation. I resigned, which is what the managers had intended all along.

These were the intolerable working conditions. I was in Rikers Island from Monday, January 30, 1995 until Thursday, February 2, 1995. The managers placed me in a maximum security area. I was not allowed to speak with anyone and there was no work for me to do. The Telecommunications Director told me that I was not there to do work for his Division. There was no telephone or computer on my desk, I was not given access to a computer and my computer password had been revoked. The transfer increased my commute time from 30 minutes to one hour and 45 minutes, which complicated my observance of the Sabbath. The Telecommunications Director forbade me kosher food in the jail cafeteria. Someone placed a swastika upon my desk. There was no choice but to resign, claim unemployment benefits and look for another job.

Did I jump or was I pushed? I would not have resigned but for the transfer to Rikers Island. The Good People told me that I should have complained about the swastika and that I had made a mistake to resign.

The local Unemployment Benefits office determined that I was disqualified from receiving benefits because of a voluntary leaving of employment without good cause. The Unemployment Benefits Judge sustained the initial determination. He denied my unemployment benefits. He decided that this was a voluntary resignation because I could have grieved the swastika. However two years later, in March 1997, the Unemployment Insurance Appeal Board rendered its decision. It overruled the initial determination and it reversed the decision of the Judge.

The Appeal Board found the transfer increased my commute time to one hour and 45 minutes and this complicated my Sabbath observance. I was alarmed to be working at a prison location. Kosher food was available for the inmates and the uniformed guards but I was specifically informed that I could not obtain any. There was no time to leave the island during my lunch break. On the last day of employment, I found a swastika on my desk, and I resigned. The Appeal Board decided that I had good cause to leave my employment.

CHAPTER THIRTY-FIVE

THE DOCTRINE OF CONSTRUCTIVE DISCHARGE

MAXWELL: You're fired.

FRAN: Fired? After all I've done, this is the thanks I get?
Oh no, you can't fire me, Maxwell Sheffield. I quit.
(She slams the door, then returns)
No, you fired me. That way I can collect unemployment.
FRAN DRESCHER.

Nanny Fran has taught the two ways by which an employee can leave his job - with or without unemployment benefits. Either he can leave his job in a way by which he can collect unemployment benefits or he can leave his job in a way by which he can not collect unemployment benefits. Unemployment benefits is only the beginning - the employee may then pursue additional claims for wrongful dismissal against the employer.

The law says that employment relationships are generally terminated by resignation or discharge. An employee voluntarily severs the relationship by resignation; the employer does so by actual discharge. ("Turner"). If the employee leaves his job because he has been fired, dismissed, discharged or terminated through no fault of his own, then the employee collects unemployment benefits. But if the employee chooses to leave, if it is a voluntary quit or a voluntary resignation, then the employee does not collect unemployment benefits.

Is the resignation truly voluntary? What if the resignation is not voluntary? What if the employer forces the employee to resign? The law calls this constructive discharge. It is also called constructive termination or constructive dismissal. Constructive discharge occurs when the employer's conduct effectively forces an employee to resign. If there is an involuntary resignation, then it is a dismissal and the employee collects unemployment benefits.

When an employee resigns, the default presumption is voluntary quit. The employee has to persuade the fact-finder, by a preponderance of the evidence, that this is not a voluntary quit but that it is a constructive discharge. If the employer can succeed in forcing the employee to resign, then the employer has placed the burden of proof upon the shoulders of the employee. The employee who resigns has an uncertain, stony and uphill climb to prove constructive discharge. He has to show unbearable working conditions, so intolerable that a reasonable person would have felt compelled to resign.

Before resigning, one first has to complain about working conditions to the employer, otherwise the employer can use failure to complain as an affirmative defense. The law says, an employer may defend itself by showing that it had a readily accessible and effective policy for reporting and resolving complaints which the plaintiff unreasonably failed to use. ("Suders").

In October 1991, I requested accommodation for Sabbath observance. Two weeks later, the managers revoked my computer password and served me disciplinary charges. The managers denied me training, they gave me inappropriate and degrading work duties, they did not invite me to the Division's office party, they gave me negative performance evaluations, they told me not to speak to co-workers and they told co-workers not to speak to me. I was shouted at and called incompetent and crazy. For three years, there was a hostile work environment, but I soldiered on and came to work on time every day. The managers transferred me to Rikers Island, the working conditions were intolerable and I resigned. This was a constructive discharge.

I complained to the Union, the EEO Officer and EEO Director, the Inspector General, the Assistant Commissioner, the Personnel Director, the City Labor Relations Director, the Commissioner for Correction, the EEOC and to the Federal Court. The harassment, discrimination and retaliation continued unabated. I complained of the harassment and retaliation and then the managers harassed and retaliated against me some more because of my complaints of harassment and retaliation.

The Systems Director wrote, "I am strongly recommending Mr. Newman's immediate dismissal." The Assistant Commissioner wrote, "actions are resuming against him now." The managers clearly intended to terminate my employment. They transferred me to Rikers Island to force me to resign.

The law says, if the employer deliberately makes an employee's working conditions so intolerable that the employee is forced into an involuntary resignation, then the employer has encompassed a constructive discharge. ("Young").

The working conditions at Rikers Island were intolerable. The transfer lengthened my commute time to one hour 45 minutes and interfered with my Sabbath observance. The Telecommunications Director told me that I could not have kosher food in the jail cafeteria. Someone placed a swastika on my desk. I resigned. The Unemployment Insurance Appeal Board decided that I had good cause to leave my employment.

Besides alleging constructive discharge, a complaint must additionally allege a tort. "This court has not and does not now recognize a cause of action in tort for abusive or wrongful discharge of an employee." ("Murphy"). I alleged that the Department had violated two Federal laws. I was a permanent tenured public servant and the managers deprived me of my property interest in my appointment without a due process hearing, contrary to Section 1983. The managers constructively discharged me because I requested accommodation for Sabbath observance, contrary to Title VII. I waited for the Court to set a trial date.

PART FIVE

TITLE VII
AND DISCRIMINATION

CHAPTER THIRTY-SIX

DEPARTMENT DID NOT REASONABLY ACCOMMODATE MY RELIGIOUS OBSERVANCE

The law requires an employer to reasonably accommodate an employee's religion if it can do so without undue hardship.
HARDISON.

In 1990, I had been leaving at 1:00 pm on Fridays for Sabbath observance and making up the time. This did not cause undue hardship to the Department. In 1991, the EEO Officer refused to accommodate my leaving at 1:00 pm on Fridays for Sabbath observance and making up the time. She did not say undue hardship. I believe that her refusal to let me leave at 1:00 pm on Fridays and make up the time was unreasonable. I believe that the Department did not make the accommodation which the law requires.

My working day on Fridays, my "tour", ended at 4:00 pm. During winter, the Sabbath arrived as early as 4:10 pm on Fridays. I needed time to travel home from work and to prepare for the Sabbath. During winter 1990-1991, the Executive Director had agreed to an accommodation by which I left work early on Friday at 1:00 pm and made up the time.

In April 1991, the first Executive Director left and a new Executive Director was appointed. In April 1991, the second Executive Director ended this accommodation for Sabbath observance. He told me that I could not leave work until 4:00 pm on Fridays. He said that he did not approve of employees working irregular hours. He did not say that it would cause undue hardship to the Department to accommodate my Sabbath observance. In October 1991, I approached the EEO officer and for seven weeks she remained silent and in November 1991, she told me that I could not leave at 1:00 pm on Friday for Sabbath observance. In 1990, the Department reasonably accommodated my Sabbath observance. From October 1991 until February 1995, when I resigned, the Department and its managers did not reasonably accommodate my Sabbath observance.

Reasonable accommodation for religious observance is Federal law. It is a legal right, not a privilege. It is not a favor to be bestowed by the managers upon employees whom the managers personally like and withheld by caprice from employees whom the managers personally dislike. The only lawful defense for denying accommodation for religious observance is undue hardship. The Department and its managers did not reasonably accommodate my Sabbath observance. At no time did the managers ever say that it would cause undue hardship to the Department to accommodate my religious observance of the Sabbath.

On October 8, 1991, I approached the EEO Officer. I requested reasonable accommodation for Sabbath observance to leave at 1:00 pm on Fridays and make up the time. I submitted a letter from my Rabbi but the EEO Officer disregarded the Rabbi's letter. She remained silent and her silence forced me to choose between either to obey the requirements of my religion, and to leave work early on Friday, or to obey the requirements of my employment, and to leave work at the end of the working day. I told the EEO Officer that if she did not respond to my request immediately, then I would have to leave on

Fridays at 1:00 pm without permission. She told me that she did not condone this kind of behavior; but she did not say that it would cause undue hardship to the Department to accommodate my observance of the Sabbath. So I left early on Fridays at 1:00 pm but without permission, without agreement and without any accommodation.

On November 27, 1991, the EEO Officer came to me and she told me that I could not leave work at 1:00 pm on Fridays and make up the time. She said that I had to stay at work until 2:00 pm on Fridays and make up the time. Permission to leave at 2:00 pm on Friday and make up the time was not reasonable accommodation because it did not give me the time I needed to travel home from work, prepare for the Sabbath and arrive on time for Synagogue services.

Two weeks after I requested accommodation for Sabbath observance, the Department brought me up on charges for walking about. But the Department took no action against the Assistant Commissioner who walked about while smoking cigarettes and who set fire to the wastepaper basket.

The Assistant Commissioner singled me out and treated me differently, and worse, than the other computer programmers. In August 1992, he told me that he had read the Rabbi's letter, and he disagreed with it. He did not restore my computer password or send me on training classes. In July 1993, the Assistant Commissioner recommended to the Commissioner that I am incompetent and that he is resuming action against me. In January 1995, he transferred me to Rikers Island without my consent. His memorandum to me did not address how he intended to accommodate my Sabbath observance.

None of the other computer programmers were ever transferred or relocated to Rikers Island. The transfer to Rikers Island increased my commute home from 30 minutes to one hour and 45 minutes and that this complicated my Sabbath observance. The real reason the Assistant Commissioner transferred me to Rikers Island was to complicate my Sabbath observance and to cause me to resign.

In October 1991, I informed the EEO Officer that I am Jewish, and I requested reasonable accommodation to observe the requirements of my religion. The Jewish religion requires adhering to a kosher diet and it forbids eating non-kosher food. Because of my Jewish religion, I only eat kosher food. The Rikers Island jail cafeteria had kosher meals readily available. The kosher meals came in frozen microwavable plastic trays, sealed under rabbinic supervision. On Monday, January 30, 1995, during my lunch break, I ate a hot kosher meal at the jail cafeteria.

The law requires the employer to reasonably accommodate an employee's religious requirements, if it can do so without undue hardship. But on Tuesday morning, the Telecommunications Director permitted me non-kosher meals at the jail cafeteria but he forbade me to eat kosher meals at the jail cafeteria. On Tuesday, January 31, 1995, in the depth of winter, after traveling to work for nearly two hours, being at work for eight hours and then traveling two hours home, I went hungry. I had not brought any food with me as I had expected to eat a kosher meal at the jail cafeteria.

The managers discriminated against me because I requested accommodation for Sabbath observance. The transfer to Rikers Island increased my commute and complicated my Sabbath observance. The Telecommunications Director told me that I was not allowed kosher meals at the jail cafeteria. But he did not say that permitting me to eat kosher meals at the jail cafeteria would cause undue hardship to the Department.

CHAPTER THIRTY-SEVEN

THE PAYROLL MANAGEMENT SYSTEM WAS A FAKE ASSIGNMENT

Who am I? Why am I here?
ADMIRAL JAMES STOCKDALE.

In September 1991, I completed the Visitors Pass system. In October 1991, I requested accommodation for Sabbath observance. Two weeks later, the managers revoked my computer password. The Department employed me as a computer programmer but, without a password, I could not do my job. I went to the EEOC, to the City Personnel Director and to the City Council President, and I complained to them that the managers had revoked my password. Three years later, the managers still had not restored my password.

In July 1993, the Systems Director recommended terminating my employment and the Assistant Commissioner told the Commissioner that I was incompetent and he was taking action against me. Since then, neither the Assistant Commissioner nor the Systems Director had met with me, not even once. In March 1994, the Executive Director gave me a corrective interview to tell me that I am unprofessional and disruptive.

In January 1995, the Assistant Commissioner relocated me to Rikers Island. He wrote that the purpose of the relocation to Rikers Island was for me to work on the Payroll Management system and that this relocation would be conducive to my success. The law says, once the employer has articulated a legitimate nondiscriminatory reason to explain his action, then it is for the employee to argue that the explanation is false or pretextual. ("McDonnell Douglas").

The Personnel Director delivered an envelope to me by hand. The envelope contained two memoranda, both dated January 13, 1995. The first memorandum was from the Assistant Commissioner. It bore the title "Work Location" and it referred to a Payroll Management system. The second memorandum was from Systems Director Waldmann. It bore the title "Department Telephone Directory Project".

The first memorandum from the Assistant Commissioner transferred or relocated me to the Telecommunications Division in Rikers Island. The memorandum said: *"The work assignments given to you involve the conversion of Payroll Management System COBOL (PMS) data into documentation usable by our systems. This information is used by the Telecommunications Division to fulfill their mandates... Mr. Douglas Waldmann has given you work assignments to complete as noted in the enclosed memorandum."*

The second memorandum from Systems Director Waldmann concerned a Telephone Directory Project. The memorandum said: *"This memo is the outline of a Telephone Directory Project which I am assigning to you. It entails developing programs to build and update files containing information for a Department Telephone Directory."*

The Assistant Commissioner's memorandum said that I would be working on a Payroll Management System. It said nothing about a Telephone Directory. Systems Director Waldmann's memorandum said that I would be working on a Telephone Directory. It said nothing about the Payroll Management System. So what work was I supposed to do? A Payroll Management System? A Telephone Directory? Both?

*

There was no Telephone Directory work for me to do in Rikers Island.

I was in Rikers Island from Monday, January 30, 1995 until Thursday, February 2, 1995. On Monday, I reported to the Telecommunications Director at Rikers Island. He did not give me any instruction concerning the Telephone Directory. I was a computer programmer. He provided me with a desk but the desk had no telephone and no computer. I asked him for access to a computer but no access was provided. Nor did he restore my computer password. Systems Director Waldmann had instructed me to develop the Telephone Directory, to "develop programs to build and update files." It is difficult to develop programs to build and update files when one does not have a computer password or have access to a computer.

No one, neither the Assistant Commissioner, nor the Systems Director nor the Telecommunications Director, met with me to give me any instructions concerning the Telephone Directory. The Telecommunications Director did not introduce me to anyone who had anything to do with the Telephone Directory. While I was at Rikers Island, no one approached me to discuss the Telephone Directory.

On Wednesday, my third day in Rikers Island, I introduced myself to the supervisor of the computer consultants. The consultant told me that his team had already completed a Telephone Directory system. The Telecommunications Director briskly walked over and interrupted us. I told him that I was engaged in Telecommunications work so I needed to speak with the consultants. The Telecommunications Director replied that I was not there to do Telecommunications work, I was not allowed in the PBX area and I was not allowed to speak with the consultants. But the Telecommunications Director arrived one moment too late and the secret was out. By the time he interrupted us, I had found out that the consultants had already completed the Telephone Directory. By instructing me to develop the Telephone Directory, Systems Director Waldmann was instructing me to do work that had already been done.

The Assistant Commissioner wrote: "You are to report to the Director of Telecommunications Division." However the Telecommunications Director told me that I did not report to him. The Telecommunications Director said that I reported to Mr. Waldmann.

This is what the Telecommunications Director wrote: *"At 2.50 pm I saw Mr. Newman in the PBX Control Room questioning Mr. Farler of Harris Corp. preventing him from doing his work. I called Mr. Newman aside and reminded him that the PBX area was off-limits and he was not permitted in the area. He said he needed to talk to Harris Corp. since he was doing Telecommunications work. I corrected and reminded him that he did not report to me or Telecommunications. His Supervisor is Mr. Doug Waldmann and his work is not Telecom and its Vendors."*

Systems Director Waldmann was located in the Information Systems Division in Manhattan. Yet the Assistant Commissioner had relocated me to the Telecommunications Division in Rikers Island. There was no point in relocating me to Rikers Island so that I could report to Mr. Waldmann, who was in Manhattan.

The Assistant Commissioner's memorandum had not said anything about a Telephone Directory. Systems Director Waldmann instructed me to develop the Telephone Directory, to "develop programs to build and update files" - without a computer password and without access to a computer. The team of consultants had already developed the Telephone Directory. There was no Telephone Directory work for me to do in Rikers Island. The Telephone Directory project was a fake assignment.

*

There was no Payroll Management work for me to do in Rikers Island.

Neither the Assistant Commissioner nor Systems Director Waldmann met with me to explain work assignments concerning the Payroll Management system or conversion of PMS data.

I was in Rikers Island from Monday, January 30, 1995 until Thursday, February 2, 1995. On Monday, I reported to the Telecommunications Director at Rikers Island. He did not tell me what data the Telecommunications Division needed to fulfill its mandates. Nor did he give me any work assignments concerning the Payroll Management system. He provided me with a desk but the desk had no telephone and no computer. I asked him for access to a computer but no access was provided. Nor did he restore my computer password.

The Assistant Commissioner had written "the work assignments involve the conversion of Payroll Management System COBOL (PMS) data...Mr. Douglas Waldmann has given you work assignments to complete as noted in the enclosed memorandum." No, not true. Systems Director Waldmann's memorandum concerned a Telephone Directory but his enclosed memorandum had not given me any work assignments involving the conversion of Payroll Management System COBOL (PMS) data.

No one, neither the Assistant Commissioner, nor the Systems Director nor the Telecommunications Director, met with me to give me any instructions concerning the Payroll Management system. The Telecommunications Director did not introduce me to anyone who had anything to do with the Payroll Management system. While I was at Rikers Island, no one approached me to discuss the Payroll Management system.

Payroll is managed by the Office of Payroll Administration, a City agency outside of the Department of Correction. The Department of Correction has a Payroll Management unit which liaises with the Office of Payroll Administration. The employees of this unit were located in the Department of Correction's Personnel Division in Manhattan - not in Telecommunications Division at Rikers Island. There was no point in relocating me to Telecommunications Division in Rikers Island to work on the Payroll Management system, when the employees of the Payroll Management unit were located in Manhattan.

The Assistant Commissioner wrote: "The work assignments given to you involve the conversion of Payroll Management System COBOL (PMS) data into documentation usable by our systems. This information is used by the Telecommunications Division to fulfill their mandates." But the Telecommunications Director did not tell me what data the Telecommunications Division needed to fulfill its mandates. He specifically told me that I did not report to him or Telecommunications and that I was not doing Telecommunications work. He wrote, "I corrected and reminded him that he did not report to me or Telecommunications. His Supervisor is Mr. Doug Waldmann and his work is not Telecom."

Payroll Management is handled by Personnel Division in Manhattan, not by Telecommunications Division in Rikers Island. Systems Director Waldmann had not given any Payroll Management work assignments to me. The Telecommunications Director told me that I was not doing work for Telecommunications Division. I had no computer password, no access to a computer, no phone, no training, no terms of reference, and nobody to speak with. The Assistant Commissioner had relocated me to Rikers Island on a fool's errand. The Payroll Management System was a fake assignment. It was a pretext to relocate me to Rikers Island.

*

The memorandum continued, *"Mr. Waldmann will evaluate your performance... We also feel that this relocation will allow you the opportunity to complete your work in an atmosphere conducive to success."*

Mr. Waldmann had shouted at me, he had given me a negative performance evaluation and he had recommended to the Assistant Commissioner, the immediate termination of my employment; so Mr. Waldmann evaluating my performance was not conducive to my success. Moreover, denying me access to a computer and denying me a computer password would not allow me to complete my work.

All of the other computer programmers worked in Information Systems Division in Manhattan and none of them had ever been transferred to Rikers Island. I wrote to the Assistant Commissioner to protest the relocation but he did not reply. Nor did he meet with me. He was taunting me and he was not interested in my success. On the contrary, he told the Commissioner that he was taking action against me. It is not credible that he transferred me to Rikers Island for the purpose of allowing me to complete my work in an atmosphere conducive to success.

Payroll Management system? False - Systems Director Waldmann did not give me any Payroll Management work assignment.

Used by Telecommunications Division? False - Telecommunications Director told me that I was not there to do Telecommunications work.

Telephone Directory? False - The consultants had already completed the Telephone Directory.

Conducive to my success? False again - The managers intended to terminate my employment.

The Department and its managers discriminated against me because I had requested accommodation for Sabbath observance. The real reason the Assistant Commissioner transferred me to Rikers Island was to lengthen my commute and complicate my Sabbath observance; and to cause me to resign.

CHAPTER THIRTY-EIGHT

PERSONALITY CONFLICT

Title VII prohibits discrimination because of religion, it prohibits retaliation because the employee has engaged in a protected activity, and it requires accommodation for religious observance. The Department employed me as a computer programmer and I completed the highly technical Visitors Pass system. But once the managers had revoked my computer password, then I could no longer perform my duties as a computer programmer. The managers gave me sham make-work and I could not do this make-work to the satisfaction of my supervisor. They gave me negative performance evaluations and they branded me incompetent.

The law says, an employer must not discriminate in training. ("Thompson"). I was employed as a computer programmer. I am Jewish, and I was not given Admins training. I requested Admins training but the Executive Director denied my request. The Assistant Commissioner gave me an IIS assignment and he told me to learn Admins from the manual. The other computer programmers were not Jewish, they worked on the IIS and they were all sent on an Admins training course while I was left behind. This is a prima facie case of failure to train because of religion.

In March 1991, the Executive Director who appointed me left the Department and a new Executive Director was appointed. Raymond Hickox, the new Executive Director, did not like me. In April 1991, he called me obnoxious. Moreover he revoked the agreement I had with the previous Executive Director concerning accommodation for Sabbath observance because, he said, he did not approve of employees working irregular hours. For the Executive Director to call me obnoxious shows animosity but it is not clear whether the animosity was because I am a Jew who observes the Sabbath, or whether because he simply disliked me.

Was there a personality conflict? The Assistant Commissioner's first words to me were that there would be no discrimination in his Department. He and the other managers ridiculed me and they subjected me to a hostile working environment but they never said that they hated Jews. The law says, a personality conflict certainly does not translate into discrimination. An employer is not required to like his employees. ("Williams"). Perhaps this hostility was not discrimination because of my religion but, rather, there was a personality conflict and the managers simply disliked me. Perhaps the managers did not send me on an Admins training course, not because I am Jewish, but because they disliked me. Is disliking an employee a legitimate nondiscriminatory reason for denying training?

From March 1991 through September 1991, I developed and completed the Visitors Pass system. The atmosphere was thin but nothing showed up on the radar. In October 1991, I requested accommodation for Sabbath observance. Two weeks later, the managers revoked my password and served me with charges. In May 1992, the Program Manager told me that I am a dead man. In June 1993, the Systems Director shouted at me that I am incompetent and crazy. The Commissioner had published a policy saying that employees are to be treated with dignity. I wrote to complain to the Commissioner that the Systems Director had not treated me with dignity but she did not reply. I could not tell whether the Department and its managers discriminated against me because of my religion or whether the managers disliked me because of a personality conflict. But the law required the Department to accommodate my Sabbath observance, whether the managers liked me or whether they disliked me.

CHAPTER THIRTY-NINE

PRIMA FACIE CASE

Nor will there ever be wanting to a prince legitimate reasons to excuse his bad faith.
MACHIAVELLI.

I made several allegations that the Department violated Title VII, Section 1983 and Civil Service law. Title VII, as amended by the Civil Rights Act of 1991, is Federal law. One section of the law prohibits discrimination because of race, color, religion, sex, or national origin. Another section prohibits retaliation for engaging in a protected activity. Section 1983 actions are analyzed in the same way as Title VII actions.

The Department and its managers discriminated against me because I observe the Sabbath. They retaliated against me because I approached the Department's EEO Officer to request accommodation for Sabbath observance. The managers singled me out and treated me differently and worse than the other computer programmers. They harbored animosity towards me and they intended to terminate my employment. They engaged in a three-year campaign of harassment against me, which culminated in the transfer to Rikers Island.

There are two kinds of evidence of discrimination, direct and circumstantial. Direct evidence of discrimination is when the employer places a sign at the factory gate saying "Whites only." The Department and its managers were too discreet to write, "We are terminating your employment because you are a Jew who observes the Sabbath." I had to fall back on circumstantial evidence. How does the employee prove discrimination when he only has circumstantial evidence, that is, indirect evidence of discrimination? He starts by bringing a prima facie case. What is a prima facie case?

"McDonnell Douglas" is the overarching framework by which a plaintiff uses circumstantial evidence to prove a Title VII violation. This framework sets out three steps. The first step is for the plaintiff, the employee, to show a "prima facie" case. The second step is for the defendant, the employer, to articulate a "legitimate nondiscriminatory reason" to explain its actions. The third step is for the plaintiff to persuade the factfinder that the proffered reason is false or "pretextual", and that the employer's action was motivated by discrimination.

The law says that when the plaintiff comes to Court without direct evidence of discrimination, then he must first establish a prima facie case. To establish a prima facie case, the plaintiff must show that each of the three or four essential conditions have been met. Each condition is called a "prong". An "adverse employment action" is an example of a prong. If an essential prong is missing, then the plaintiff has failed to establish a prima facie case and the Court will dismiss the case. Choosing which prongs to present is like selecting dishes from a restaurant menu. There are different kinds of complaints, for example dismissal, constructive discharge, failure to appoint, failure to promote, demotion, training, hostile work environment, sexual harassment. Legal precedent has provided each kind of complaint with its own set of prongs, which the employee will present to establish a prima facie case. One Title VII action may contain multiple prima facie allegations.

*

The law says that the employee proves religious discrimination first by establishing a prima facie case. (1) He has a bona fide religious belief that conflicts with an employment requirement; (2) he informed the employer of this belief; (3) he was disciplined for failure to comply with the conflicting employment requirement. ("Philbrook").

This is my prima facie case for discrimination because of religion. (1) I am Jewish and I observe the Sabbath; (2) I approached the Department's EEO Officer to request accommodation for Sabbath observance; (3) The managers transferred me to Rikers Island; (4) I was the only computer programmer ever to have been transferred to Rikers Island; (5) The transfer to Rikers Island increased my commute time and interfered with my Sabbath observance.

*

The law says that the employee proves retaliation first by establishing a prima facie case. (1) participation in a protected activity; (2) the defendant's knowledge of the protected activity; (3) an adverse employment action; and (4) a causal connection between the protected activity and the adverse employment action. ("Zann Kwan").

This is my prima facie case for retaliation. (1) I approached the Department's EEO Officer to request accommodation for Sabbath observance; (2) Two weeks later, the managers revoked my computer password and served me with disciplinary charges.

*

The law says, a tenured employee protected by the full panoply of rights accorded by the Civil Service Law must be given a hearing before termination or any other disciplinary action is taken. ("Soto").

This is my prima facie case for wrongful disciplinary action. (1) I was a tenured civil servant; (2) The Assistant Commissioner relocated me to Rikers Island with the intention of taking action against me; (3) This relocation was an adverse action which changed the terms and conditions of my employment; (4) There was no civil service disciplinary hearing prior to relocation.

*

The law says, there cannot be a "transfer" of an employee without his consent in writing. Transfer means the change of a permanent employee from a position under the jurisdiction of one appointing authority to a position under the jurisdiction of another appointing authority. ("Vrooman").

This is my prima facie case for wrongful transfer. (1) I was a permanent tenured civil servant; (2) My appointment was to the Information Services Division; (3) The Assistant Commissioner ordered me to report to the Director of Telecommunications Division; (4) Each division, Information Systems Division and Telecommunications Division, is an appointing authority, each with its own director with authority to manage the division and to appoint employees; (5) I did not consent to the transfer.

*

The law says, if the employer deliberately makes an employee's working conditions so intolerable that the employee is forced into an involuntary resignation, then the employer has encompassed a constructive discharge. A tenured public employee has a constitutionally protected property interest in his employment. A public employer obviously cannot avoid its constitutional obligation to provide due process by the simple expedient of forcing involuntary "resignations." ("Young," "Loudermill," "Stone").

This is my prima facie case for deprivation of property interest without due process of law. (1) I was a tenured public employee with a constitutionally protected property interest in my employment; (2) The Department and its managers intended to terminate my employment; (3) They transferred me to Rikers Island to force me to resign; (4) There was no due process hearing; (5) The Unemployment Insurance Appeal Board decided that I had good cause to leave my employment.

This is my prima facie case for constructive discharge because of religion. (1) I approached the Department's EEO Officer to request accommodation for Sabbath observance; (2) The Department and its managers intended to terminate my employment; (3) They transferred me to Rikers Island to force me to resign; (4) The Unemployment Insurance Appeal Board found that the transfer to a remote facility complicated my Sabbath observance and certainly hindered my ability to comply with aspects of my religious beliefs; (5) The Appeal Board decided that I had good cause to leave my employment.

*

"Bona fide religious belief." I am Jewish and I observe the Sabbath.

"Protected activity." I approached the Department's EEO Officer. I told her that I am Jewish. I requested accommodation for Sabbath observance. I asked to leave at 1:00 pm on Fridays and make up the time. I requested the same accommodation as the Department had granted me the previous year. I told the EEO Officer that I had already been to see the current Executive Director but that he had remained silent. To approach the EEO Officer to request accommodation for Sabbath observance is to engage in a protected activity.

"Defendant's knowledge of the protected activity." The EEO Officer was employed by the Department of Correction to handle EEO matters. The Department and its managers knew because I told the EEO Officer.

"Adverse employment action." The Department and its managers revoked my computer password and served me with disciplinary charges because I requested accommodation for Sabbath observance. By revoking my computer password they prevented me from performing the duties for which I had been appointed. They brought me up on disciplinary charges. I took three months of sick leave. The managers launched a three-year campaign of harassment and they visited multiple adverse employment actions upon me, including the transfer to Rikers Island.

"Causal connection." The managers had known of my personal use of the computer back in April 1991 but they remained silent. On October 8, 1991, I approached the EEO Officer. On October 23, 1991, the Department and its managers revoked my computer password and they charged me with personal use of the computer. The law says that the temporal proximity can establish a causal connection between the protected activity and the unlawful employment action in the retaliation context. The law says that a passage of less than three weeks is significant enough to constitute evidence of a causal connection for the purposes of satisfying a prima facie case of retaliation. ("Mickey"). Only two weeks passed between when I approached the EEO Officer to request accommodation for Sabbath observance and when the Department and its managers took action against me. This close proximity of time supports the inference that the managers revoked my computer password and charged me with personal use of the computer to retaliate against me because I had requested accommodation for Sabbath observance.

The law says that a causal connection between the protected activity and the adverse employment action can also be established through evidence of disparate treatment of employees who engaged in similar conduct. ("Sumner"). I walked about and the Department served me with disciplinary charges. The Assistant Commissioner walked about, smoked cigarettes and set fire to the wastepaper basket, but the Department did not serve him with disciplinary charges for walking about. Nor did the Department bring him up on charges for setting fire to the wastepaper basket. The Department and its managers did not apply discipline even-handedly. They had been more strict with me than they had been with the Assistant Commissioner. The Department and its managers discriminated against me because I requested accommodation for Sabbath observance.

The law says, if the plaintiff establishes a prima facie case, a presumption of discrimination is created and the burden shifts to the employer to articulate a "legitimate, nondiscriminatory reason" for the adverse employment action. This is the second step in the "McDonnell Douglas" framework. In three memoranda, the Department and its managers articulated their reasons to explain their actions. They said that my Sabbath observance was being accommodated; I was incompetent and had done absolutely no work; the relocation to Rikers Island was for me to work on the Payroll Management system and this relocation would be conducive to my success.

In litigating a Title VII complaint, the second step is for the defendants to refute a prima facie case of discrimination by articulating a legitimate nondiscriminatory reason. The third step is for the plaintiff to persuade the factfinder that the proffered reason is false or "pretextual", and that the employer's action was motivated by discrimination. The Payroll Management system was a fake assignment. It was a pretext to transfer me to Rikers Island. When I arrived at Rikers Island, the Department and its managers did not accommodate my observances of Sabbath and of kosher food. There was nothing about the atmosphere of Rikers Island that was conducive to success.

CHAPTER FORTY

CAMPAIGN OF DISCRIMINATION AND RETALIATION

The law says, the ultimate burden of persuading the trier of fact that the defendant intentionally discriminated against the plaintiff remains at all times with the plaintiff.

HICKS.

This is my narrative by which I attempt to persuade the factfinder that the Department and its managers discriminated against me because I approached the EEO Officer to request accommodation for Sabbath observance. This is where I tell how the Department and its managers transferred me to Rikers Island and caused me to resign.

In October 1991, the clocks changed and I approached the EEO Officer to request reasonable accommodation for Sabbath observance. I asked to leave early on Friday at 1:00 pm and make up the time. This is the same accommodation that had been granted in 1990. Two weeks later the managers revoked my password and served me with disciplinary charges. For six months the managers had known that I had made personal use of the computer but they acquiesced in silence. There was no warning. Only two weeks passed between when I approached the EEO Officer to request accommodation for Sabbath observance and when the Department and its managers took action against me.

This close proximity of time supports the inference that the managers revoked my computer password and that they charged me with personal use of the computer to retaliate against me because I had requested accommodation for Sabbath observance.

The EEO Officer remained silent for seven weeks before addressing my request and for these seven weeks the Department did not accommodate my Sabbath observance. On the seventh week the EEO Officer told me that I could not leave work on Fridays until 2:00 pm and make up the time. She shorted me by an hour. Permission to leave at 2:00 pm on Friday and make up the time was not reasonable accommodation because it did not give me the time I needed to travel home from work, prepare for the Sabbath and arrive at the Synagogue on time for Sabbath services. The EEO Officer did not say that it would cause undue hardship to the Department for me to leave work on Friday 1:00 pm and make up the time.

The law requires an employer to reasonably accommodate an employee's religion if it can do so without undue hardship. ("Hardison"). Reasonable accommodation is a legal right, not a privilege. It is not a favor to be bestowed by the managers upon employees whom the managers personally like and withheld by caprice from employees whom the managers personally dislike. The managers did not say undue hardship. They offended the law both by retaliating against me because I approached the EEO officer and by not reasonably accommodating my Sabbath observance.

For three years, the managers treated me differently, and worse, than they treated the other computer programmers. There was an avalanche of abuse and discriminatory actions taken against me. The Department and its managers segregated me from the other computer programmers; they did not reasonably accommodate my Sabbath observance; they discriminated against me because of my religion; they retaliated against me because I requested accommodation for Sabbath observance, they revoked my computer password; they brought me up on charges; they denied me training; I was not invited to the office party; they intended to terminate my employment; they gave me inappropriate and degrading work assignments; they attempted to demote me; they disregarded the Arbitrator's decision and gave me no credit for completing the Visitors Pass system; they gave me false performance evaluations; they gave me a corrective interview; they shouted at me; they did not allow me to speak with co-workers and co-workers were not allowed to speak with me; they did not investigate my complaints; they subjected me to a hostile working environment; they transferred me to Rikers Island.

In June 1992, Commissioner Catherine Abate wrote to the City Council President saying that she takes all complaints of employment discrimination very seriously and that she was making every effort to resolve the issues. But she was indifferent to my complaints and she did not take them seriously.

In July 1993, the Assistant Commissioner told the Commissioner that he was taking action against me. The Commissioner knew and approved of action taken against me by her managers. She did nothing to resolve the issues and she took no corrective action. Three years passed since the managers revoked my computer password and it was never restored. The harassment and discrimination continued unabated.

Rikers Island is a maximum security area. The transfer increased my commute time home and it complicated my observance of the Sabbath and my observance of kosher food. None of the other computer programmers had ever been relocated to Rikers Island. The managers said that they relocated me to Rikers Island to develop the Telephone Directory, or the Payroll Management system data conversion for Telecommunications Division to fulfill its mandates. I had no computer password and I was not given access to a computer. The team of consultants had already developed the Telephone Directory and there was no Telephone Directory work for me to do in Rikers Island. Nor was I given any Payroll Management work assignments. The Telecommunications Director told me that I was not doing work for Telecommunications Division. The Telephone Directory and the Payroll Management data conversion were both fake assignments given for the pretext of relocating me to Rikers Island.

The managers engaged in a three-year campaign of harassment against me because I requested accommodation for Sabbath observance. When I arrived at Rikers Island, I faced unbearable working conditions. The managers refused to accommodate my religious observance. Within one week of the transfer to Rikers Island, there were three matters of religious discrimination: the extended commute hindered my Sabbath observance, the Telecommunications Director forbade me kosher food in the jail cafeteria and there was a swastika on my desk. The Department did not have an effective policy for reporting and resolving complaints and I could not complain about the swastika because of retaliation. The Unemployment Benefits Appeal Board found that there had been a transfer to a remote facility which complicated my observance of the Sabbath and that, when I found the swastika upon my desk, I had good cause to leave my employment.

In February 1995, I complained to the Personnel Director about antisemitism. There was no reply from the Department. The managers were concerned that I ate kosher food at the jail cafeteria, and they forbade me to do so. But they were not concerned that an employee of over four years of service had resigned because of antisemitism.

CHAPTER FORTY-ONE

UNEMPLOYMENT BENEFITS APPEAL BOARD DECIDES THAT I LEFT MY EMPLOYMENT FOR GOOD CAUSE

After I resigned from the Department of Correction, I applied for unemployment benefits. The local Unemployment Benefits Office decided that this was a voluntary quit and it denied my application. I appealed the decision of the local office.

In April 1995, an Unemployment Benefits hearing took place. The name of the Judge assigned to my case was Stephen Ambrecht. I came to the hearing to pursue my claim for unemployment benefits. The Union did not send a representative to accompany me. I hired an attorney to represent me. The Department of Correction did not send a representative to contest my claim.

I told the Unemployment Benefits Judge that my Sabbath observance had not been reasonably accommodated and that I had filed a complaint in Federal Court, that the transfer to Rikers Island had increased my travel time each way from 30 minutes to one hour and 45 minutes, and that this complicated my Sabbath observance. I told the Judge that I felt alarmed to work in a maximum security area, that the Department did not provide me with access to a computer, that the Telecommunications Director did not permit me to eat kosher food at the jail cafeteria and that someone placed a swastika upon my desk. The Judge summarized my testimony and he awarded me unemployment benefits.

After the Unemployment Benefits Judge mailed his decision to the parties, the Department of Correction then contacted the Unemployment Benefits Office to request that the decision be vacated as the Department had not received notification of the hearing. The Unemployment Benefits Rules provide for strict time limits and more than 20 days had elapsed since the Judge had mailed his decision. Nevertheless, the Judge vacated his decision and granted the Department's application for a new hearing.

The Unemployment Benefits Judge ordered a new hearing. This meant that I had the inconvenience of having to make two separate appearances and of having to testify twice. My attorney had to accompany me twice. It also meant that the Assistant Commissioner had the advantage of arriving at the second hearing having already read the Judge's summary of my testimony, the testimony which I had given at the first hearing, while I had the disadvantage of arriving at the second hearing without knowing in advance what the Assistant Commissioner was going to say.

In July 1995, a second unemployment benefits hearing was held. I came again to the hearing to pursue my claim for unemployment benefits. This time the Assistant Commissioner attended the hearing. He appeared as a witness for the Department of Correction to contest my claim for unemployment benefits. He was accompanied by a City representative. The Union did not send a representative to accompany me. The Judge at the second hearing was the same Judge as at the first hearing.

In the second hearing, the Unemployment Benefits Judge asked me whether I had complained about the swastika before I resigned. I replied that I had not complained about the swastika because of retaliation. I told him that the Collective Bargaining Agreement does not provide for grieving a swastika and that I had already complained to the EEO Director, to the EEOC and to the Court. I told him that the managers had harassed me and retaliated against me for over three years because I had made complaints, that I had written a letter of resignation complaining of antisemitism but there was no reply.

The Assistant Commissioner told the Unemployment Benefits Judge that the Department of Correction has a policy of zero tolerance for antisemitism and that he and the Department always encourage employees to come forward and to make their complaints. He recited a list of organizations that I should have approached, non-profit organizations which handle complaints of antisemitism and of civil rights violations. Instead of being outraged that someone had placed the swastika upon my desk, the Assistant Commissioner expressed his indignation that I had resigned without first coming to him to complain about the swastika. He told the Judge that if I had complained about the swastika, then my complaint would have been investigated.

I had sent my letter of resignation by certified delivery and the USPS returned the signed and dated mail receipt card. There was no reply. The Assistant Commissioner told the Unemployment Benefits Judge that the Department had not received my letter of resignation. Following the second hearing, the Judge mailed his decision. He found as a fact that my letter of resignation had not been received. He determined that this was a voluntary resignation without good cause because I could have grieved the swastika. He decided that unemployment benefits should be denied.

The Unemployment Benefits Judge, he was well-spoken and smartly-dressed, a man of wisdom and understanding. Undoubtedly he had a law degree. Upon the request of the Assistant Commissioner, the Judge both vacated his original decision and he held a second hearing. After the hearing was complete, my wife and I overheard the Judge speak to the Assistant Commissioner. He addressed him by his first name. Indeed! So the Judge and the Assistant Commissioner were already on familiar first name terms and perhaps they were old friends! The Judge should have told me that he was already acquainted with the Assistant Commissioner. In the two years that I had known him, the Assistant Commissioner and I had never once addressed each other by our first names. Had the Judge and the Assistant Commissioner perhaps engaged in an ex parte discussion of this case? Perhaps this was the reason why the Judge vacated his original decision and held a second hearing.

The law says that the signed certified mail return receipt card creates a presumption of receipt. ("Fodor"). The Unemployment Benefits Judge disregarded the law. I believe that the Judge was prejudiced against me. He failed to declare that he was personally familiar with the Assistant Commissioner. He decided that it was a voluntary resignation without good cause as I should have grieved the swastika. He denied my application for unemployment benefits. I hired a law firm to write my appeal.

The local Unemployment Benefits office determined that I was disqualified from receiving benefits because of a voluntary leaving of employment without good cause. The Unemployment Benefits Judge sustained the initial determination. He denied my unemployment benefits. He decided that this was a voluntary resignation because I could have grieved the swastika. However two years later, in March 1997, the Unemployment Insurance Appeal Board rendered its decision. It overruled the initial determination and it reversed the decision of the Judge.

The Appeal Board found the transfer increased my commute time to one hour and 45 minutes and this complicated my Sabbath observance. I was alarmed to be working at a prison location. Kosher food was available for the inmates and the uniformed guards but I was specifically informed that I could not obtain any. There was no time to leave the island during my lunch break. On the last day of employment, I found a swastika on my desk, and I resigned. The Appeal Board decided that I had good cause to leave my employment.

STATE OF NEW YORK
UNEMPLOYMENT INSURANCE APPEAL BOARD
P.O. BOX 15126
ALBANY, NY 12212-5126
(518) 402-0205

MICHAEL R. CUEVAS
CHAIRMAN

ARTHUR A. STRAUSS
ALLEN P. CAPPELLI
KENNETH M. MACKINTOSH
LEWIS ZANKEL
MEMBERS

JOSEPH P. KEARNEY
EXECUTIVE DIRECTOR

ROBERT A. LORENZO
CHIEF ADMINISTRATIVE LAW JUDGE

Mailed and Filed: MAR 2 6 1997

IN THE MATTER OF:

Appeal Board No. 453069

CYRIL S NEWMAN

NYC DEPT OF CORRECTION
PERSONNEL DEPT
225 BROADWAY
NEW YORK NY 10004

NYC DEPT. OF PERSONNEL
U.I. DIVISION, 20TH FLOOR
2 WASHINGTON STREET
NEW YORK NY 10004

BART L. NASON, P.C.
ATT: NICK TCUMBEKIS
420 LEXINGTON AVE, SUITE 620
NEW YORK NY 10017

DANIEL KAISER
405 PARK AVENUE, 15TH FLOOR
NEW YORK NY 10022

A.S.O. - Appeals Section
Department of Labor Office: 517

A.L.J. Case No. 095-19800
S.S.A. or E.R. No.

PLEASE TAKE NOTICE that within THIRTY DAYS after the mailing of this decision, the commissioner or any other party affected thereby who appeared at the appeal before the board may appeal questions of law involved in such decision to the Appellate Division of the Supreme Court, Third Department. Written notice of such appeal should be mailed to the Unemployment Insurance Appeal Board, P.O. Box 15126, Albany, New York 12212-5126 within THIRTY DAYS after the mailing of this decision.

TOME NOTA que durante el periodo de TREINTA DIAS a partir de la fecha que la decision fue enviada por correo, el comisionado u otra parte afectada que testifico frente a la junta puede apelar preguntas con respecto a la ley en cuanto a la decision a la Division de Apelaciones de la Corte Suprema, Tercer Departamento. Aviso por escrito de la apelacion debe ser enviado a Unemployment Insurance Appeal Board, P.O. Box 15126, Albany, New York 12212-5126 durante TREINTA DIAS a partir de la fecha que la decision fue enviada por correo.

DECISION OF THE BOARD

PRESENT: Allen P. Cappelli, Arthur A. Strauss MEMBERS

By initial determination of the local office, the claimant was disqualified from receiving benefits, effective February 3, 1995, because of a voluntary leaving of employment without good cause The claimant requested a hearing.

The Administrative Law Judge held hearings at which all parties were accorded a full opportunity to be heard and at which testimony was taken. There were appearances on behalf of the claimant and of the employer. By decision filed July 14, 1995, the Administrative Law Judge sustained the initial determination.

The claimant appealed the Judge's decision to the Appeal Board. In connection with its review of the case, the Board considered the arguments contained in the written statements submitted.

Based on the record and testimony in this case, the Board makes the following

EXHIBIT 16. *Unemployment Benefits Appeal Board decision that I left my employment for good cause, dated March 26, 1997.*

Appeal Board No. 453069 Page 2

<u>FINDINGS OF FACT</u>: The claimant, a computer operator, worked for the New York City Department of Correction for about five years until February 2, 1995. Until January 30, 1995 the claimant had been working at an office location in Manhattan which was about a half hour commute from the claimant's home. During the course of his employment the claimant had disputes with the employer concerning the effect of the job on his ability to fulfill his religious obligations as an observant Jew.. As these matters were not resolved to the claimant's satisfaction, he had filed a lawsuit in Federal Court charging the employer with discrimination. Subsequently the employer filed disciplinary charges against the claimant.

On January 30, 1995, the employer transferred the claimant to a secured inmate facility on Riker's Island. This increased the time of claimant's commute to about 1 and ¾ hours each way, which complicated this ability to accommodate his Friday Sabbath observance. He was also alarmed to be working at a prison location and found that although Kosher food was available for the inmate population as well as uniformed guards, he was specifically informed that he could not obtain any. It was not possible for the claimant to leave the island within the time constraints of his lunch break. On his last day of employment the claimant found a swastika on his desk. He thereupon resigned from his employment.

<u>OPINION</u>: The evidence establishes that the claimant left his employment after a series of events which caused him to believe that the employer was discriminating against him because of his religious beliefs. While we do not hold that the evidence in this case establishes that the claimant's belief was correct, it does convince us that the claimant's perception was genuine and that the transfer to a remote facility certainly hindered his ability to comply with aspects of his religious beliefs. Under these circumstances, when the claimant found that someone had placed a swastika on his desk, we conclude that he had good cause to leave his employment

<u>DECISION</u>: The initial determination of is overruled.

The decision of the Administrative Law Judge is reversed.

Allen P. Cappelli, MEMBER

AT:UR

Arthur A. Strauss, MEMBER

EXHIBIT 16. *Continued.*

PART SIX

SETTLEMENT

CHAPTER FORTY-TWO

JURY TRIAL

The jury eagerly wrote down all three dates
on their slates, and then added them up,
and reduced the answer to shillings and pence.
LEWIS CARROLL.

Had the Department discriminated against me because of my religion? Had the Department reasonably accommodated my Sabbath observance? Had the Department retaliated against me because I had been to see the EEO Officer? Why did the Department revoke my computer password? Had the Department caused me to be out sick for three months? Had the working conditions been unbearable? Would it have been undue hardship to allow me a kosher meal in the jail cafeteria, when kosher food was available to other employees? Had the Department constructively discharged me? Had there been a hearing prior to the transfer to Rikers Island? Had the Department behaved outrageously? Should the Jury award damages - how much?

Both Title VII and Section 1983 provide for Jury trial in Federal Court. There are six jurors in a civil action. I believe that six honest jurors, good and true, randomly selected from the general public, can better reach a fair and impartial verdict than can one judge sitting alone. In every other part of the process, the corporation is stronger than the employee. Assuming that the Jury is indeed randomly selected from the general population and not stacked, for example by race, then I believe that the Jury is chaotic and irrational and that each trial and each Jury is unique. Juries only see what they want to see. No one knows whom the Jury will favor. Maybe they will decide for the employee because they feel that the employee has a confident posture and a trustworthy face.

I believe that in a civil court, the Jury is the one part of the judicial system that the wealthy corporations and the powerful government agencies are unable to buy, control, influence or even predict. Appealing to the Jury is like rolling dice and neither side has an advantage. It is the irrationality of the Jury that makes them impervious to manipulation. Precisely because of their irrationality, one can hope that a Jury will reach a fair and impartial verdict. The Jury guarantees the impartiality of the Court. Before the Jury, the weak can defeat the strong.

The parties will study appellate court decisions to understand controlling law. In New York City, this means looking closely at precedents and decisions made by the New York State Court of Appeals, the Second Circuit Court of Appeals and by the US Supreme Court. If the defendants move for summary judgment and the District Court dismisses the case, then the plaintiff may appeal the dismissal but to appeal a dismissal may cost thousands of dollars. If the District Court does not dismiss the case, or if the Appeals Court reverses the judge's decision, then the case goes to Jury.

Although Jury trials are the stuff of Hollywood, only one percent of civil cases are actually tried by Jury. (Smith and MacQueen). Some cases are dismissed and the rest settle. Some cases do not settle until voir dire. What matters is for the employee to establish his right to address the Jury, a Jury that has not yet been empaneled, on such and such a future date. The trial date creates an urgency for serious settlement discussion to commence. Opposing sides stand together, together they stare deep down into the cost and uncertainty of a trial. Then they settle. Nothing else in the world quite so concentrates the mind of the Corporation Counsel of the City of New York as the imminent prospect of a million dollar Jury verdict.

CHAPTER FORTY-THREE

CASH SETTLEMENT

You have stolen my dreams.
GRETA THUNBERG.

In October 1991, I approached the EEO Officer. In September 1993, I brought my complaint to Court. I had been out sick for three months because of the harassment and retaliation. The Corporation Counsel of the City of New York denied my allegations. In February 1995, the Department transferred me to Rikers Island. I resigned. I added new allegations to my complaint still pending with the Court. I complained of transfer to Rikers Island, interference with my Sabbath observance, denial of kosher food, failure to provide a computer and the swastika. I complained that the Department and its managers had constructively terminated my employment. The Corporation Counsel again denied my allegations. The City argued that the disciplinary charges, the performance evaluations, corrective interview and assignment to Rikers Island were all given in good faith for business reasons. In March 1997, the Unemployment Benefits Appeal Board decided that I had left my employment for good cause.

In May 1997, Senator Moynihan wrote to the Second Circuit to request a trial date. A new judge was appointed to try my case and a trial date was set. The City Corporation Counsel could have moved for summary judgment. Instead it chose to settle my complaint for cash. I hired an attorney who negotiated the settlement. My annual salary had been $40,000. The City offered a cash settlement of $65,000. I accepted the City's offer. The settlement was selflessly and generously paid for by the New York City taxpayer. I was a New York City taxpayer. Because the settlement was income, I had to pay tax to the City on the settlement. I was not reinstated to my job as a Computer Associate Software at the Department of Correction. Nor would I have wished to return to the Department of Correction. I would only have returned to the City if I had been promoted to a different City agency.

The City provided free legal representation for Mr. Waldmann. He did not have to pay a penny out of his own pocket. He never had to pay back to the City the money that the City paid to me to settle the damages which he had caused. Nor did he ever apologize for the misery that he caused me. Why should the New York City taxpayer underwrite the malfeasance of City managers? For three years, Mr. Waldmann harassed me and he got away with it. A year after I resigned, the Department promoted him to Deputy Commissioner.

How could the managers abuse me for over three years and derail my civil service career? Why was there no oversight or accountability? Where was the Inspector General and the Department of Investigation? Where was the EEOC? Where was the Court? The Court did not protect me from being transferred to Rikers Island. I have lost confidence in the Court and in the protection of the law.

There was no catharsis. The City paid a cash settlement. I got the money and the case is settled but I will never be made whole. This case took a huge chunk of my life and my wife suffered with me. There are scars that will never heal. For me there was no happy ending.

UNITED STATES DISTRICT COURT
SOUTHERN DISTRICT OF NEW YORK
---x

CYRIL STEPHEN NEWMAN,

Plaintiff,

- against -

CATHERINE ABATE, RAYMOND HICKCOX, AND DOUGLAS WALDMAN, individually and as employees of of the New York City Department of Correction, THE NEW YORK CITY DEPARTMENT OF CORRECTION, and THE CITY OF NEW YORK,

Defendants.

---x

STIPULATION AND ORDER OF SETTLEMENT AND <u>DISCONTINUANCE</u>

93 Civ. 6155 (MP)

WHEREAS, plaintiff commenced this action by filing a summons and complaint on or about September 1, 1993 alleging that the defendants discriminated and retaliated against him;

WHEREAS, defendants have denied any and all liability arising out of plaintiff's allegations;

WHEREAS, the parties now desire to resolve the issues raised in this litigation, without further proceedings and without admitting any fault or liability;

WHEREAS, no party herein is an infant or incompetent for whom a committee has been appointed; and

WHEREAS, there is no person not a party who has interest in the subject matter of this action;

EXHIBIT 17. *Settlement with City Corporation Counsel, dated May 8, 1997.*

NOW, THEREFORE, IT IS HEREBY STIPULATED AND AGREED, by and between the attorneys for the respective parties herein, as follows:

1. The above-referenced action is hereby dismissed, with prejudice, and without costs, expenses, or fees in excess of the amount specified in paragraph "2" below.

2. Defendants agree not to make plaintiff's personnel file available to any person or body other than an agency of the City of New York or other public law enforcement agency without plaintiff's written consent, and pay plaintiff the sum of $65,000 (sixty-five thousand dollars) in full satisfaction of all claims, including claims for costs, expenses and attorney's fees. In consideration therefor, plaintiff agrees to withdraw with prejudice the instant complaint, and release all defendants, their successors and assigns, all present or former employees or agents of the Department of Correction of the City of New York, and the City of New York from any and all liability, claims, or rights of action plaintiff had or might have had arising out of the events alleged herein, including claims for costs, expenses and attorney's fees.

3. Plaintiff shall execute and deliver to defendants' attorney all documents necessary to effect this settlement, including, without limitation, a release based on the terms of paragraph "2" above and an Affidavit of No Liens.

4. Nothing contained herein shall be deemed to be an admission by any of the defendants that it has in any manner or way violated plaintiff's rights, or the rights of any other person or entity, as defined in the constitutions, statutes, ordinances, rules or regulations of the United States, the State of New York, or the City of New York or any other rules, regulations or bylaws of any department or subdivision of the City of New York. This

EXHIBIT 17. *Continued.*

stipulation shall not be admissible in, nor is it related to, any other litigation or settlement negotiations.

5. Nothing contained herein shall be deemed to constitute a policy or practice of the City of New York.

6. This Stipulation and Order contains all the terms and conditions agreed upon by the parties hereto, and no oral agreement entered into at any time nor any written agreement entered into prior to the execution of this Stipulation and Order regarding the subject matter of the instant proceeding shall be deemed to exist, or to bind the parties hereto, or to vary the terms and conditions contained herein.

Dated: New York, New York
May 8, 1997

JOEL FIELD
Attorney for Plaintiff
230 Park Avenue, 23rd Floor
New York, New York 10169
(212) 687-5522

By: [signature]
JOEL FIELD

PAUL A. CROTTY
Corporation Counsel of the
City of New York
Attorney for Defendants
100 Church Street, Room 2-123
New York, N.Y. 10007
(212) 788-0920

By: [signature]
JUDITH C. McCARTHY (JM-0222)
Assistant Corporation Counsel

SO ORDERED:

____
U.S.D.J.

____
DATED

EXHIBIT 17. *Continued.*

CHAPTER FORTY-FOUR

MY PERSONNEL FILE

He that filches from me my good name robs me
of that which not enriches him and makes me poor indeed.
SHAKESPEARE.

Disciplinary charges had been brought against me that I raised my voice to my supervisor, made personal use of the computer and walked about. According to the plea agreement, the Department had agreed to expunge the charges from my record after six months. More than six months had elapsed since the agreement was signed. I have never been shown my personnel file, to read my personnel file would mean filing a Freedom of Information application, and I do not know whether the Department kept its promise to expunge the charges.

I suppose that the contents of my personnel file have been digitally scanned into a computer file. This file will be held on disk and stored in City archives for a hundred years and it will include the disciplinary charges, the memorandum saying that I am incompetent, the negative performance evaluations and a notation that a corrective interview had been given.

The performance evaluations stated that my performance was unacceptable and I had not completed any assignments. A performance evaluation once written cannot be reviewed, appealed or grieved. So the negative performance evaluations remained in my file. The Assistant Commissioner wrote a memorandum to the Commissioner which called me incompetent and which said that I did absolutely no work. The Executive Director gave me a corrective interview saying that I was unprofessional and disruptive. All of this would be recorded in my personnel file. There was no way to set the record straight. I resigned for good cause because of the transfer to the Rikers Island jail and the swastika. The managers will have excluded this from my personnel file.

After reviewing my personnel file, as edited by the managers, the reader might well conclude that I was an incompetent, unprofessional and disruptive employee whose performance had been unacceptable and who had not completed any assignments. The personnel file will tell the reader that I walked about but it will not tell the reader that I completed the Visitors Pass system. The City paid cash to settle my complaint of employment discrimination and, according to the settlement, the personnel file is sealed.

CHAPTER FORTY-FIVE

JOBS FOR THE BOYS

I seen my opportunities and I took 'em...
This civil service law is the biggest fraud of the age...
We stood as we have always stood, for reward - it's the
men that won the victory. They call that the spoils system.
PLUNKITT.

The New York City taxpayer is paying top dollar for hotshot managers with sonorous job titles; managers whose skills, merit and competency have never been tested.

The purpose of a civil service system is to provide government with the administrative machinery to execute its policies. The civil service bureaucracy is impartial. It favors neither one party nor another party, neither one policy nor another policy. The task of the civil service is to bring speed, efficiency, economy and integrity to public administration. Civil servants carry out the requirements and policies of their agency and each new administration comes into office with confidence in its administrative machinery. Competent government is meritocratic and civil service employees are chosen by talent and merit. Merit is identified by civil service examination. In order that civil servants can properly perform their duties, they must be allowed to work under the supervision of qualified managers, free from political interference.

For many years, New York City had a civil service examination system with a level playing field. The competitive examination system opens opportunity of lower middle-class employment to people without political connection. Everyone had an equal opportunity of passing or failing the exam. The exams contained multiple-choice questions which were intended to seek out skills, ability, aptitude and competency. The purpose of the examination had been to pass people with merit and to fail people without merit. But this all changed. The City reverted from a civil service system to the spoils system.

In a spoils system, the employee has been appointed for some reason which has nothing to do with merit; such as secret societies, drinking buddies, family friends or romantic relationships. Plunkitt argues that without a spoils system there cannot be patriotism. Patriotism is nice but under the spoils system, the City of New York pays out wages without confidence that the people it employs will bring to the job the skills which the job requires. Managers and supervisors are hired lacking basic skills. The City is short-changed and the taxpayers do not receive the quality of services to which they are entitled and for which they have paid.

The civil service system is based upon merit. Under the civil service system, a person pays cash to take a civil service exam. Perhaps he passes the exam. City Personnel Department investigates and validates his skills and experience, and it adds his name to the list of qualified candidates. He is interviewed and appointed from the list to his new City agency, he serves a year of probation and he receives a satisfactory performance evaluation. This way, the City has confidence that the people it employs can competently perform their duties. A permanent civil servant is eligible to take promotional examinations.

Once a New York City employee, who has been hired from the civil service list, has completed his year of probation, he then becomes a tenured and permanent civil servant. He is protected both by the Fourteenth Amendment and by Civil Service law. This protection means that he enjoys a presumption of competency in his position, he has a constitutional due process property interest in his employment and he may not be terminated, or subjected to any disciplinary action, without a hearing.

It is proverbial that, just as one rotten apple can spoil a barrel, so can one rotten employee ruin an organization. One manager who lacks basic skills can also ruin an organization. He can deflect blame by placing blame on a subordinate. It takes a civil service system to make sure that only skilled employees are hired and to make sure that only experienced employees with a track record of proven skills are promoted to positions in which they can supervise subordinates. The hearing process protects competent employees from rotten supervisors. The civil service system guarantees the integrity of the machinery of government. This benefits not just the individual civil servant but society as a whole. Without a civil service system - waste, incompetence and corruption.

So why a spoils system? There is a danger that a small, well-organized, well-educated elite clique of senior civil servants could evolve into an entrenched caste which would promote an agenda antagonistic to the aspirations of the electorate and of its representatives. This danger would be averted by a spoils system. The spoils system rotates ordinary people into the high reaches of government and so keeps the administration of government close to the people. After an election a new set of people takes control of the government. In principle, no one is in control beyond the next election.

At best, the spoils system has the virtue of importing new ideas, new ways of seeing things, new methods and techniques that were not developed from within the civil service hierarchy. There may well be a role for consultants with up-to-date skills. It would be reasonable for a commissioner to bring in one or two trusted campaign advisers who are personally loyal to him; advisers with imagination, original ideas and graduate degrees. But the careers of experienced civil servants should not be subjected to the whims and caprice of unqualified and grandiose hacks with political connections.

Furtively, without public debate, the old discredited Tammany spoils system was restored and the professional nonpartisan meritocratic civil service system was phased out. The City circumvented recruitment from the civil service list by hiring from the Mayor's Talent Bank, now known as the Mayor's Office of Appointments, and by giving contracts to consulting companies. Friends of friends were appointed. The City Personnel Department was replaced by the Department for Citywide Administrative Services. Employees who had passed the civil service exams were supervised, evaluated and disciplined by managers who had been appointed through the spoils system and who had not passed the civil service exams. The Department of Investigation found that the Department of Correction employed correction officers who had criminal convictions.

The City has continued to schedule civil service examinations because they are a useful source of revenue. People without political connections paid money to take the civil service exams, but they were rarely appointed from the lists. Few supervisors have been promoted from the rank and file and few City employees have been appointed from a civil service list. Instead, appointment at all levels, managerial and clerical, have been made through the spoils system, without regard to merit or ability. Jobs were churned. Employees left and new employees were hired through the spoils system. Years would pass between scheduling the examinations and publishing the lists. The lists were then retired and new examinations were scheduled. Except for the uniformed employees, firefighters, correction officers and police officers, few people keep their jobs for long.

Today the civil service system and the spoils system co-exist. There is a hybrid spoils and civil service system, a chimera. Civil Service law has not been repealed and it remains in the statute books. The City employs both civil servants, employees appointed from the civil service list, and "provisionals", employees-at-will. The employees are supervised by managers who have been appointed through the spoils system. Plunkitt would be proud.

The Department of Correction is run on favoritism, cronyism and patronage. The managers were dishonest, abusive, unskilled, unqualified and incompetent. There were too many chiefs and not enough computer programmers. Why did the Information Systems Division need a Director for Systems Development, an Executive Director for Management Information Systems and an Assistant Commissioner for Technical Development and Project Management, two other managers and four secretaries, when there were only seven computer programmers?

Does a galleon go to sea with a crew of seven sailors, two captains, three admirals and four cabin boys? Does an army division go to war with seven soldiers, two generals, three field marshals and four batmen? Not one of these three managers held a college degree in computers. Not one of these managers had passed a civil service computer exam. These managers had not in any way proven their competency. They had no measurable skills, no proven track record and no concrete accomplishments. All they ever did was to attend management meetings. Here, in the Information Systems

Division, not one of these managers had ever written a computer program. Not one of these managers could have written a computer program if his life depended upon it. The Information System Division could have performed just as well with four secretaries, seven computer programmers, two managers, a Hatter, a March Hare and a Dormouse.

In March 1993, the Commissioner addressed the City Council Finance Committee. She told the Committee that better management and computerization was saving nearly $100 million at the Department of Correction. She credited part of the savings to the Inmate Information System which she said had started coming on-line. Shortly before the Commissioner addressed the City Council Finance Committee, the State Comptroller's office had been auditing the IIS System. While the Commissioner had been boasting upon the Inmate Information System, the State Comptroller's office wrote that the IIS System was unsatisfactory and that the users had no confidence in it. The State Comptroller's office declared that City funds had been misspent.

The Department of Correction is a New York City agency which operates under New York State Correction law. It is charged with enforcement of the law. Yet the Department tolerates harassment and discrimination. The employment discrimination laws exist theoretically in the statute books. But in practice, in the workplace, the managers flouted the laws because the EEOC did not investigate my complaint and the Court did not enforce the law.

What is a civil service job worth? I passed the Civil Service computer exam, was appointed from the list, completed probation and was awarded my Master's degree in Public Administration. It astonishes me, not that I resigned from a supposedly secure civil service job, but that for three years I was exposed to harassment and discrimination and that I was alone. I completed the Visitors Pass system and the managers revoked my computer password, charged me with walking about and said I was incompetent. Where was the Union? Where was the EEOC? Where was the Court? Why was I alone with no one to champion me? An employee who completes a highly technical assignment on his own with little supervision should be feted as a hero. He should not be harassed, hounded out of his job and forced to resign.

CHAPTER FORTY-SIX

THE UNION BETRAYED ME

You don't get me I'm part of the Union.
STRAWBS.

The Union makes us strong.
RALPH CHAPLIN.

The name of my Union was DC37. My Union had multiple locals and each local had a president. My local was 2627 and the President of my Union local was Robert Crilly.

In March 1991, the Program Manager, instructed me to develop a Visitors Pass system. This assignment was difficult. I approached the Union. I spoke to the Union President and Representative both together but they refused to file my grievance on my behalf pursuant to the Collective Bargaining Agreement and I had no standing to invoke the grievance procedure of the Collective Bargaining Agreement. After several months I filed the grievance on my own pursuant to the Department's Rules and Regulations. The Arbitrator decided that the Visitors Pass system was highly technical and out of title and that I deserved an award for out of title work. The Arbitrator wrote that it was "unfortunate that Grievant was not encouraged enough by the comments made by his union representative."

In October 1991, the Department served disciplinary charges on me and recommended that I would be suspended without pay from my employment for forty-five days, fifteen days for each charge. I met with the Union President and Representative both together. They told me that I was guilty as charged. They told me that I should not have made personal use of the computer. In particular, they could not defend my raising my voice to my supervisor. I told them that I did not raise my voice to my supervisor. They said they knew that I raised my voice to my supervisor because the Department had witnesses.

The Union's defense should have been that I was an innocent victim of management retaliation, but instead, the Union's defense was that this was my first offense and that forty-five days suspension without pay was a violation of the doctrine of progressive discipline. The Union President and Representative had not given sound advice. They recommended that I plead guilty to one of the charges in exchange for the other two charges being dropped, and serve only fifteen days of suspension. They also recommended that I abandon my out of title Visitors Pass grievance as part of a plea bargain. The Union Representative gave me no hope. She was too eager to plead me guilty. She had already judged my case and decided against me. I rejected the advice of the Union. I insisted on appearing before the Office of Administrative Trials and Hearings to face trial. In April 1993, the disciplinary charges were adjourned contemplating dismissal.

I complained to the Union that the managers had revoked my computer password. I was a computer programmer but, for three years, I had to come to work without having a computer password. I complained to the Union that I was denied computer training given to the other employees. I complained to the Union that the managers instructed me to document old obsolete computer programs and that this work was inappropriate and degrading. I complained to the Union about the negative performance evaluations. The Union Representative explained to me that my supervisors gave me negative performance evaluations because they were not satisfied with my work. The Union failed to protect my rights in the workplace.

I complained to the EEOC. The Department's EEO Director directed me to appear before her office. The Executive Director directed me to attend a corrective interview. The Union Representative refused to accompany me on my meeting with the EEOC. She refused to accompany me on my meeting with the EEO Director, and she used an expletive, and she refused to accompany me on my meeting with the Executive Director at the corrective interview. So I met with the EEOC, the EEO Director and the Executive Director, attending each meeting on my own, without Union representation.

Civil Service law prohibits transfer without consent but the Union Representative laughed at me when I complained to her about the transfer to Rikers Island. The Union did nothing to oppose the transfer to Rikers Island. I had to attend the Unemployment Benefits hearing, and win my own appeal, without Union representation.

For over three years, the Department of Correction and its managers had violated my rights as an employee in the workplace. The Union never tried to help me. I was supposedly represented by the Union but at every moment, I had to represent myself. Being a member of a Union and representing oneself is like keeping a dog and doing one's own barking. Could I have sued the Union for failure to represent? Before going to court, one would first have to prosecute a complaint against the Union with the National Labor Relations Board. This procedure would divert my attention away from the complaint against the Department of Correction. I reached my own settlement with the City, without Union representation.

CHAPTER FORTY-SEVEN

JUSTICE DELAYED IS JUSTICE DENIED

The sword comes into the world because of justice delayed and because of justice perverted.
PIRKEI AVOS.

In October 1991, I approached the Department's EEO Officer to request accommodation for Sabbath observance. Two weeks later, the Department and its managers revoked my computer password and they served me with disciplinary charges. In December 1991, I complained to the EEOC but the EEOC did not investigate my complaints. The managers gave me negative performance evaluations, branded me as incompetent and intended to terminate my employment. In August 1993, the EEOC issued a Notice of Right to Sue and it closed the case.

I filed my complaint with the Court in September 1993. There was no escape from the harassment. I cried out to the Court, help me, help me! The Court remained silent. The Court is there to enforce the law and it should have tried my case. The Court failed me. It kept its doors locked, it failed to protect me, it remained silent and it did not set a trial date. The silence of the Court emboldened the managers and they learned that they could bait me without consequence. The Department and its managers repeatedly broke the law and violated my rights.

They continued to discriminate against me because I observe the Sabbath; and the Court remained silent.

In January 1995, while I was waiting for the Court to set a trial date, the Assistant Commissioner transferred me to Rikers Island to complicate my Sabbath observance and he forced me to resign. The law could not protect me from the harassment because the Court did not enforce the law. I was defenseless. The Court remained silent even as the Department and its managers transferred me to Rikers Island. There was nowhere else left to grieve or complain.

The relocation or transfer to Rikers Island increased my commute from 30 minutes to one hour and 45 minutes and this complicated my Sabbath observance. The Payroll Management assignment was a fake assignment, there was no access to a computer and no work for me to do at Rikers Island. This was a maximum security area. While I was at Rikers Island, the Telecommunications Director forbade me to eat kosher food at the jail cafeteria. Someone placed a swastika upon my desk. I resigned. All this happened while my case lay pending in Federal Court, but the Court did not protect me from the harassment and discrimination. Justice delayed was assuredly justice denied.

The law says, a permanent civil servant has a Fourteenth Amendment property interest in his employment. He is entitled to a due process pre-termination hearing and the opportunity to tell his side of the story. The Assistant Commissioner wrote that he was taking action against me and then he took the law into his own hands. He transferred me to Rikers Island, while my complaint of employment discrimination was still pending before the Court. He transferred me to Rikers Island without meeting with me, without my consent and without a hearing.

I had been a permanent civil servant and I enjoyed the protection of Civil Service law. Civil Service law is quite clear - no transfer without consent and no action without a hearing. The law says that a tenured employee protected by the full panoply of rights accorded by the Civil Service Law must be given a hearing before termination or any other disciplinary action is taken. ("Soto"). I complained to the Court but the Court locked its doors, it remained silent and it did not set a trial date to hear my complaint. The law cannot protect me unless the Court is there to enforce the law.

In February 1995, I applied for unemployment benefits. In March 1997, the Unemployment Benefits Appeal Board decided that I had been transferred to Rikers Island; that this was a transfer to a maximum security area; that the transfer to Rikers Island increased my commute home from 30 minutes to one hour and 45 minutes; that this was a transfer to a remote facility which complicated my observance of the Sabbath; and that, when I found the swastika on my desk, I had good cause to leave my employment.

The Department and its managers forced me to resign and they cheated me of my constitutional right to a due process pre-termination hearing. The Good People did nothing to help me and they told me that it was a mistake for me to resign. The Unemployment Benefits Appeal Board decided that I had good cause to leave my employment, it awarded me unemployment benefits, but it had no jurisdiction over the loss of my civil service job. That was a matter for the Court. I had filed my complaint with the Court in September 1993. My case lay pending before the Court, but the Court remained silent and it would not set a trial date.

Discovery was complete, the case had long been ready for trial but the Court sat on my complaint for more than three years, from September 1993 until May 1997, and it did not set a trial date. During this time I had passed a civil service promotional examination. Had the case settled while I was still employed by the Department of Correction, then the settlement agreement could have stipulated both cash, to compensate my damages, and also a promotion to a new City agency. But the Court sat on my complaint and it kept its doors locked. The managers forced me to resign. Once I had resigned, then I was no longer on the City payroll and so it was no longer possible to promote me to a new City agency.

The Court remained silent. It did not set a trial date. The managers took advantage of the Court's silence to transfer me to Rikers Island to force me to resign. The relocation to Rikers Island increased my commute home and it complicated my Sabbath observance. Civil Service law prohibits transfer without consent or action without hearing, but the Court remained silent. The Department of Correction and its managers cheated me out of my job, my letter of recommendation, my civil service pension and my promotion. They were able to do this because the Court remained silent and it failed to protect me.

In vain did the New York State Senate pass the Civil Service Law to prevent employees from being relocated or transferred without consent or hearing. In vain did Congress pass Title VII, and the Civil Rights Act of 1991, to protect employees from discrimination. In vain did the states ratify the Fourteenth Amendment to guarantee that no person shall be deprived of property without due process. When the Court remains silent and fails to enforce the law, then there is no protection of the law.

The law requires the employee to complain to the EEOC within 180 days and the EEOC has 180 days to investigate before providing a right-to-sue letter. Once the employee has received his right-to-sue letter from the EEOC, the law only allows him 90 days to bring his complaint to Court. Since the law is so rushing me with deadlines, then why cannot the law be more demanding from the Court? Why should the Court take more than three years and still not give me a trial date!

I filed my complaint with the Court in September 1993. When a customer buys a table from a furniture store, then he expects the furniture store to set a delivery date and to deliver the table and chairs to his house on that date. When a plaintiff files a complaint, then he expects the Court to set a trial date. Why should a Federal Court be held to a lesser standard than a furniture store? Not only did the Department cheat me of my pre-termination hearing, the Court did not allow me a post-termination hearing. I was a permanent civil servant, I was forced out of my job and the only hearing given to me was the unemployment benefits hearing.

I wrote to the Court to request a trial date. The Court broke its silence but, instead of setting a trial date, the clerk wrote back, "Never write to this Court again." I approached my US Senator, Daniel Patrick Moynihan. He wrote to the Second Circuit to request a trial date and, in May 1997, the Second Circuit appointed a new judge to hear the case. But it was too late. More than three years had passed since I had brought my complaint to Court. I had long since resigned and there was nothing left to get out of the settlement but cold cash.

This case had started in October 1991 and it ended in May 1997. This case had gone on for longer than the Second World War and it had gone all the way, from the EEO Officer to the Inspector General, to the City Council Member, to the City Council President and to the Commissioner, to the EEOC and to the Court, and then to the Senator. I would like to see rules concerning setting dates for civil trials so that a judge, by silence, indifference and inertia, cannot deny a litigant his day in court. Had my Senator not requested a trial date, then perhaps even today I would still be waiting for my day in court.

Judges are supposed to judge and to uphold the rule of law. Judges are supposed to judge fairly and impartially, with righteousness, wisdom and dispatch. They are not appointed so that they can sit aloof in judicial silence and solitude, solemnly watching the world go by, while collecting their salaries. The Court remained silent. I paid a filing fee so that I could have a trial by Jury. The Court cashed my filing fee but it did not set a trial date. I filed my complaint with the Court in September 1993. It was not until May 1997, after the Senator wrote to the Second Circuit and a new Judge was appointed, that a trial date was set. Until May 1997, I never saw the Judge. The Constitution provides for speedy trials in criminal prosecutions but it makes no provision for speed in civil trials. Trial dates are set at the discretion of the Court.

Citizens should not take the law into their own hands. Conversely the Court is expected to enforce the law. The Court should have intervened to protect me from the harassment and from the transfer to Rikers Island. What is the point of laws about employment discrimination when the EEOC is out to lunch and the Court keeps its doors locked! This was a do-nothing Court. I paid good money to the Courthouse to file my complaint, so as to try my case and to address the Jury, but the Court was not keeping to its end of the deal. It cheated me of my filing fee. The Court is there to uphold the rule of law. When judges do not judge, then there is no rule of law. When there is no rule of law, then there is no protection of the law.

CHAPTER FORTY-EIGHT

PEOPLE WHO HELPED ME

City Personnel Director, Douglas White and City Council President, Seth Diamond wrote to the Commissioner to tell her that I had made serious allegations. U.S. Senator Daniel Patrick Moynihan wrote to the Second Circuit to request a trial date. City Council Member Stanley Michels wrote to the Commissioner for Investigation to request an investigation into the Program Manager's residency. Deputy Commissioner for Trials Allyson Lewis-Smith told me that I had been treated unfairly. She guided me towards having my civil service disciplinary hearing held under the auspices of OATH rather than under the Union grievance procedure.

These are the lawyers who helped me. Michelle Jacobowitz, who defended me at the OATH pre-trial conference. The charges were adjourned. Jeffrey Schwartz, who represented me at the Visitors Pass arbitration. The Arbitrator found that I had completed the Visitors Pass system. This was a highly technical out of title assignment. John Upton, who wrote out and filed my complaint to Federal Court. This complaint resulted in a cash settlement. Daniel Kaiser, who accompanied me to the Unemployment Benefits hearing. The Judge's decision was to deny my unemployment benefits. Nick Toumbekis, who wrote and filed my appeal to the Unemployment Benefit Appeals Board. The Appeal Board reversed the Judge's decision and it found that I had left my employment for good cause and that I was entitled to unemployment benefits. Joel Field, who negotiated the cash settlement with the City of New York Corporation Counsel.

Barbara, my wife, was my most loyal supporter. She was my only supporter. She was the one who arranged the meeting with the Deputy Commissioner for Trials. She was there at the pretrial OATH conference when the disciplinary charges were adjourned. She was there when I won at the out of title arbitration. She was with me when I hired the law firm to write out my complaint, serve summonses and file my complaint with the Court. A few days before I was due to report for work there, she came with me to travel to Rikers Island to check out the route and traveling time. After the Telecommunications Director forbade me to have kosher food at the cafeteria, my wife packed cold lunches for me.

When I found the swastika on my desk, my wife and her family insisted that I had to resign. My wife came with me to the Unemployment Benefit hearing. She made the phone calls to bring my case to the attention of the Senator. My wife was with me during this ordeal when the Union, the EEOC, the Court and all the Good People turned their back on me.

CHAPTER FORTY-NINE

WHERE THEY WENT

It is not in our hands to explain why
the wicked prosper, or why the righteous suffer.
PIRKEI AVOS.

The Commissioner for Correction floated majestically over the Department like a Thanksgiving Parade balloon. But Rudy Giuliani defeated the incumbent Mayor, David Dinkins. A new Mayor had been elected who did not owe the Commissioner any favors. The Mayor's office cut her loose because of an inmate riot on her watch. She ran for New York State Attorney General and was defeated. In May 2014, she unfortunately passed away. In "The Villager" obituary, Catherine Abate was "a shining star of the New York criminal justice system and a great advocate for justice for all...We are all better off because of her."

The next Commissioner was about to become United States Secretary for Homeland Security but he was a crook. He was convicted of felony corruption and he was sent to prison. The Inspector General was fired for being too cozy with the crooked Commissioner. He brought legal action for wrongful dismissal and he collected a settlement. The President of my Union local was indicted for embezzlement of Union funds. Both he and the Union Representative have passed away.

The Personnel Director resigned in 2014 after the Department of Investigation found that the Personnel

Division hired correction officers who had criminal convictions or who were members of gangs. Even after he resigned, the Department of Investigation found that the Personnel Division continued to recruit health care workers for the jails without first checking their background.

In 1996, the Assistant Commissioner was transferred from Department of Correction to Administration for Children's Services, where he stayed for two years. In 1997, New York State signed a $177 million contract with Andersen Consulting to design the software for the "Connections" computer information system. The Assistant Commissioner had overall responsibility for the Connections system. In 1998, he left ACS to work for Anderson Consulting. In 2007, the Department of Investigation examined the death of Nixzmary Brown, and ten other children, and it was sharply critical of the Connections system.

Mr. Douglas E. Waldmann, the Director for Systems Development, was promoted to Deputy Commissioner. In October 2002, he retired from the Department. The Department held a dinner in his honor and announced that he was "trading in his years of computer expertise for a life of ease."

The Program Manager resigned after being confronted by the Department of Investigation concerning his address. The Telecommunications Director kept his job.

The Honorable Judge, she who would not give me a trial date, has since passed away. In February 2020, Colleen McMahone, Chief Judge, SDNY wrote, "It is with a heavy heart, that the Southern District of New York advises you of the passing of Senior Federal District Judge Deborah A. Batts." In October, 2001, an oil portrait of Judge Batts was unveiled at Harvard Law School. The attorney who defended the City against my action became a Federal Magistrate Judge. However Senator Moynihan, Council Member Stanley Michels and attorney Joel Field have passed away.

After I resigned from the Department of Correction, I never again worked in the public sector and I was never able to make use of my Master's degree in Public Administration. I returned to the private sector. I worked as a computer programmer and then I became a computer consultant and worked on several short-term assignments. My favorite assignment was working for Marathon in Findlay, Ohio. Then I played piano at the New Yorker Hotel, Nevada Smith's and Percy's Pub. I wrote some songs and placed two albums on YouTube and Spotify.

PART SEVEN

NOTES

WHAT THE LAW SAYS

Congress shall make no law respecting an establishment of religion or prohibiting the free exercise thereof, or abridging the freedom of speech or of the press, or the right of the people peaceably to assemble and to petition the government for a redress of grievances.

US Constitution, First Amendment.

No state shall make or enforce any law which shall abridge the privileges or immunities of citizens of the United States; nor shall any state deprive any person of life, liberty, or property, without due process of law; nor deny to any person within its jurisdiction the equal protection of the laws.

US Constitution, Fourteenth Amendment.

Every person who, under color of any statute, ordinance, regulation, custom, or usage, of any State or Territory or the District of Columbia, subjects, or causes to be subjected, any citizen of the United States or other person within the jurisdiction thereof to the deprivation of any rights, privileges, or immunities secured by the Constitution and laws, shall be liable to the party injured in an action at law, suit in equity, or other proper proceeding for redress.

42 U.S.C. Section 1983.

This is what Title VII says:

(d) Training programs

It shall be an unlawful employment practice for any employer, labor organization, or joint labor-management committee controlling apprenticeship or other training or retraining, including on-the-job training programs to discriminate against any individual because of his race, color, religion, sex, or national origin in admission to, or employment in, any program established to provide apprenticeship or other training.

(j) The term "religion" includes all aspects of religious observance and practice, as well as belief, unless an employer demonstrates that he is unable to reasonably accommodate to an employee's or prospective employee's religious observance or practice without undue hardship on the conduct of the employer's business.

a) Discrimination for making charges, testifying, assisting, or participating in enforcement proceedings.

It shall be an unlawful employment practice for an employer to discriminate against any of his employees or applicants for employment, for an employment agency, or joint labor-management committee controlling apprenticeship or other training or retraining, including on-the-job training programs, to discriminate against any individual, or for a labor organization to discriminate against any member thereof or applicant for membership, because he has opposed any practice made an unlawful employment practice by this subchapter, or because he has made a charge, testified, assisted, or participated in any manner in an investigation, proceeding, or hearing under this subchapter.

(m)Impermissible consideration of race, color, religion, sex, or national origin in employment practices.

Except as otherwise provided in this subchapter, an unlawful employment practice is established when the complaining party demonstrates that race, color, religion, sex, or national origin was a motivating factor for any employment practice, even though other factors also motivated the practice.

Title VII of the Civil Rights Act of 1964 (Title VII), 42 U.S.C. section 2000e et seq as amended.

This is what the EEOC says.

The U.S. Equal Employment Opportunity Commission (EEOC) is responsible for enforcing federal laws that make it illegal to discriminate against a job applicant or an employee because of the person's race, color, religion, sex (including pregnancy, gender identity, and sexual orientation), national origin, age (40 or older), disability or genetic information. It is also illegal to discriminate against a person because the person complained about discrimination, filed a charge of discrimination, or participated in an employment discrimination investigation or lawsuit...it is the EEOC's job to investigate the matter to determine whether there is reasonable cause to believe that discrimination has occurred...The EEO laws prohibit punishing job applicants or employees for asserting their rights to be free from employment discrimination including harassment. Asserting these EEO rights is called "protected activity," and it can take many forms. For example, it is unlawful to retaliate against applicants or employees for requesting accommodation of a disability or for a religious practice...The EEO laws prohibit punishing job applicants or employees for asserting their rights to be free from employment discrimination including harassment. Asserting these EEO rights is called "protected activity," and it can take many forms. For example, it is unlawful to retaliate against applicants or employees for requesting accommodation of a disability or for a religious practice...The anti-discrimination laws give you a limited amount of time to file a charge of discrimination. In general, you need to file a charge within 180 calendar days from the day the discrimination took place. Once you receive a Notice of Right to Sue, you must file your lawsuit within 90 days. This deadline is set by law. If you don't file in time, you may be prevented from going forward with your lawsuit.

EEOC statement.

EEOC Religious Discrimination Guidelines, No. 641 403:263: The EEOC approves flexible scheduling; the use of lunch hours in exchange for early departure and permitting an employee to make up time lost due to the observance of religious practices.

This is what New York Civil Service law says.

1. Removal and other disciplinary action. A person described in paragraph (a) or paragraph (b), or paragraph (c), or paragraph (d), or paragraph (e) of this subdivision shall not be removed or otherwise subjected to any disciplinary penalty provided in this section except for incompetency or misconduct shown after a hearing upon stated charges pursuant to this section.

New York Civil Service Law section 75.

2. (a) A public employer shall not dismiss or take other disciplinary or other adverse personnel action against a public employee regarding the employee's employment because the employee discloses to a governmental body information...

(d) "Personnel action" shall mean an action affecting compensation, appointment, promotion, transfer, assignment, reassignment, reinstatement or evaluation of performance.

New York Civil Service Law section 75-B.

No employee shall be transferred without his or her consent except as provided in subdivision six or seven of this section or upon the transfer of functions as provided in subdivision two of this section.

New York Civil Service Law section 78.

This is the Vrooman case which addresses the transfer of a civil servant.

The Court finds that the resolution of the issue before it involves a pure question of law involving statutory interpretations and, therefore, exhaustion of administrative remedies is not required...It is undisputed that the Utica and Marcy Psychiatric Centers are two distinct and separate facilities (Mental Hygiene Law, 1.03, subd 6; see, also, Mental Hygiene Law, 7.17, subd [b]). Each facility has as its "chief executive officer" a director appointed by the commissioner (Mental Hygiene Law, 7.21, subd [a]). Each director has administrative power to "appoint and remove * * * such officers and employees of the facility * * * as are necessary for its efficient administration" (Mental Hygiene Law, 7.21, subd [a]). The statute also empowers the director to "manage the facility and administer its personnel system"...Civil Service Rules ("Every transfer shall require the consent, in writing, of the transferee * * * and the approval of the Civil Service Department") (4 NYCRR 5.1[a][4]). It is clear that there cannot be a "transfer" of an employee without his consent in writing and the approval of the Civil Service Department. "(1) The term transfer means the change, without further examination, of a permanent employee from a position under the jurisdiction of one appointing authority to a position under the jurisdiction of another appointing authority or to a position in a different title in the same or a higher salary grade under the jurisdiction of the same appointing authority. The "appointing authority" is defined in subdivision 9 of section 2 of the Civil Service Law as "the officer, commissioner or body having the power of appointment to subordinate positions."

Matter of Vrooman v Prevost, 80 AD2d 933, 934

A tenured employee protected by the full panoply of rights accorded by the Civil Service Law must be given a hearing before termination or any other disciplinary action is taken (Civil Service Law section 75).

Matter of Soto v. Koehler, 171 AD 2d 567 - NY: Appellate Div., 1st Dept. 1991

The tenured public employee is entitled to oral or written notice of the charges against him, an explanation of the employer's evidence, and an opportunity to present his side of the story...An essential principle of due process is that a deprivation of life, liberty, or property "be preceded by notice and opportunity for hearing appropriate to the nature of the case." Mullane v. Central Hanover Bank & Trust Co., 339 U. S. 306, 313 (1950). We have described "the root requirement" of the Due Process Clause as being "that an individual be given an opportunity for a hearing before he is deprived of any significant property interest."[7] Boddie v. Connecticut, 401 U. S. 371, 379 (1971) (emphasis in original); see Bell v. Burson, 402 U. S. 535, 542 (1971). This principle requires "some kind of a hearing" prior to the discharge of an employee who has a constitutionally protected property interest in his employment. Board of Regents v. Roth, 408 U. S., at 569-570; Perry v. Sindermann, 408 U. S. 593, 599 (1972).

Cleveland Bd. of Ed. v. Loudermill, 470 US 532 - Supreme Court 1985

Where an employment is for an indefinite term it is presumed to be a hiring at will which may be freely terminated by either party at any time for any reason or even for no reason...This court has not and does not now recognize a cause of action in tort for abusive or wrongful discharge of an employee; such recognition must await action of the Legislature.

Murphy v. Am. Home Prod, 58 NY 2d 293 - NY: Court of Appeals 1983

Employment relationships are generally terminated by resignation or discharge. An employee voluntarily severs the relationship by resignation; the employer does so by actual discharge. Constructive discharge occurs when the employer's conduct effectively forces an employee to resign...The doctrine of constructive discharge addresses such employer-attempted "end runs" around wrongful discharge.

Turner v. Anheuser-Busch, Inc., 876 P. 2d 1022 - Cal: Supreme Court 1994

The general rule is that if the employer deliberately makes an employee's working conditions so intolerable that the employee is forced into an involuntary resignation, then the employer has encompassed a constructive discharge and is as liable for any illegal conduct involved therein as if it had formally discharged the aggrieved employee.

Young v. Southwestern Savings and Loan Association, 509 F. 2d 140 - Court of Appeals, 5th Circuit 1975

To establish "constructive discharge," the plaintiff must make a further showing: She must show that the abusive working environment became so intolerable that her resignation qualified as a fitting response. An employer may defend against such a claim by showing both (1) that it had installed a readily accessible and effective policy for reporting and resolving complaints of sexual harassment, and (2) that the plaintiff unreasonably failed to avail herself of that employer-provided preventive or remedial apparatus. This affirmative defense will not be available to the employer, however, if the plaintiff quits in reasonable response to an employer-sanctioned adverse action officially changing her employment status or situation, for example, a humiliating demotion, extreme cut in pay, or transfer to a position in which she would face unbearable working conditions...so intolerable that a reasonable person would have felt compelled to resign.

Pennsylvania State Police v. Suders, 542 US 129 - Supreme Court 2004

A claimant has the "responsibility to do whatever is necessary and reasonable in order to remain employed."

Brady v. Board of Review, 704 A. 2d 547 - NJ: Supreme Court 1997.

The petitioner's claim that he never received the notice is insufficient to rebut the presumption of receipt created by the signed certified mail return receipt card.

Matter of Fodor v. MBNA America Bank NA, 34 AD 3d 473 (2006) 823 N.Y.S.2d 353.

A Seventh-Day Adventist could not be denied unemployment compensation benefits by South Carolina because she refused to work on Saturday, her Sabbath.

Sherbert v. Verner, 374 US 398 - Supreme Court 1963

The complainant in a Title VII trial must carry the initial burden under the statute of establishing a prima facie case of racial discrimination. This may be done by showing (i) that he belongs to a racial minority; (ii) that he applied and was qualified for a job for which the employer was seeking applicants; (iii) that, despite his qualifications, he was rejected; and (iv) that, after his rejection, the position remained open and the employer continued to seek applicants from persons of complainant's qualifications...The burden then must shift to the employer to articulate some legitimate, nondiscriminatory reason for the employee's rejection.

McDonnell Douglas Corp. v. Green, 411 US 792 - Supreme Court 1973

Under the first step of the McDonnell Douglas framework, the plaintiff must establish a prima facie case of retaliation by showing 1) "participation in a protected activity"; 2) the defendant's knowledge of the protected activity; 3) "an adverse employment action"; and 4) "a causal connection between the protected activity and the adverse employment action.

Zann Kwan v. Andalex Group LLC, 737 F. 3d 834 - Court of Appeals, 2nd Circuit 2013

A plaintiff in a [Title VII] case makes out a prima facie case of religious discrimination by proving: (1) he or she has a bona fide religious belief that conflicts with an employment requirement; (2) he or she informed the employer of this belief; (3) he or she was disciplined for failure to comply with the conflicting employment requirement.

Ansonia Bd. of Ed. v. Philbrook, 479 US 60 - Supreme Court 1986

Temporal proximity can establish a causal connection between the protected activity and the unlawful employment action in the retaliation context...Where the temporal proximity between the protected activity and the adverse employment action is acutely near in time, that close proximity is deemed indirect evidence such as to permit an inference of retaliation to arise... the passage of less than three weeks between [the employer's] receipt of the charges and the adverse actions gives rise to an inference of discrimination...temporal proximity between the events is significant enough to constitute evidence of a causal connection for the purposes of satisfying a prima facie case of retaliation.

Mickey v. Zeidler Tool and Die Co., 516 F. 3d 516 - Court of Appeals, 6th Circuit 2008

The causal connection between the protected activity and the adverse employment action can be established indirectly with circumstantial evidence, for example, by showing that the protected activity was followed by discriminatory treatment or through evidence of disparate treatment of employees who engaged in similar conduct or directly through evidence of retaliatory animus.

Sumner v. US Postal Service, 899 F. 2d 203 - Court of Appeals, 2nd Circuit 1990

First, the plaintiff has the burden of proving by the preponderance of the evidence a prima facie case of discrimination. Second, if the plaintiff succeeds in proving the prima facie case, the burden shifts to the defendant "to articulate some legitimate, nondiscriminatory reason for the employee's rejection." Third, should the defendant carry this burden, the plaintiff must then have an opportunity to prove by a preponderance of the evidence that the legitimate reasons offered by the defendant were not its true reasons, but were a pretext for discrimination.

Texas Dept. of Community Affairs v. Burdine, 450 US 248 - Supreme Court 1981

To establish a prima facie case of discriminatory denial of training, a plaintiff must show that: (1) the plaintiff is a member of a protected class; (2) the defendant provided training to its employees; (3) the plaintiff was eligible for the training; and (4) the plaintiff was not provided training under circumstances giving rise to an inference of discrimination.

Thompson v. Potomac Electric Power Co., 312 F. 3d 645 - Court of Appeals, 4th Circuit 2002

Under the McDonnell Douglas framework, the plaintiff must first establish a prima facie case of discrimination. If the plaintiff establishes a prima facie case, a presumption of discrimination is created and the burden shifts to the employer to articulate a "legitimate, nondiscriminatory reason" for the adverse employment action. In order to show pretext, the plaintiff must show both that the employer's explanation was false, and that discrimination was the real reason for his decision. The ultimate burden of persuading the trier of fact that the defendant intentionally discriminated against the plaintiff remains at all times with the plaintiff.

St. Mary's Honor Center v. Hicks, 509 US 502 - Supreme Court 1993

[t]his personality conflict generated antipathy and professional incompatibility which might have made it more difficult for the plaintiff to perform. But this certainly does not translate into discrimination. An employer is not required to like his employees.

Williams v. Cerberonics, Inc., 871 F. 2d 452 - Court of Appeals, 4th Circuit 1989

The laudable practice of evaluating employees is to be encouraged...The performance review is a vehicle for informing the employee of what management expects, how the employee measures up, and what he or she needs to do to obtain wage increases, promotions or other recognition. Thus, the primary recipient and beneficiary of the communication is the employee.

Jensen v. Hewlett-Packard Co., 14 Cal. App. 4th 958 - Cal: Court of Appeal, 4th Appellate Dist., 3rd Div. 1993

A poor performance evaluation could very well deter a reasonable worker from complaining...A negative evaluation, or the threat of a negative evaluation, while not an adverse employment action that affects terms and conditions of employment, might dissuade a reasonable worker from making or supporting a charge of discrimination.

Vega v. Hempstead Union Free School Dist., 801 F. 3d 72 - Court of Appeals, 2nd Circuit 2015

Constructive discharge occurs when the working conditions deteriorate, as a result of discrimination, to the point that they become sufficiently extraordinary and egregious to overcome the normal motivation of a competent, diligent, and reasonable employee to remain on the job to earn a livelihood and to serve his or her employer.

Brooks v. City of San Mateo, 229 F. 3d 917 - Court of Appeals, 9th Circuit 2000

We refuse to transmute such ordinary workplace disagreements between individuals of different races into actionable race discrimination...It is not our province to decide whether the reason was wise, fair, or even correct, ultimately, so long as it truly was the reason for the plaintiff's termination...It is the perception of the decision maker which is relevant, not the self-assessment of the plaintiff...Our sole concern is whether the reason for which the defendant discharged the plaintiff was discriminatory... And no court sits to arbitrate mere differences of opinion between employees and their supervisors.

Hawkins v. PepsiCo, Inc., 203 F. 3d 274 - Court of Appeals, 4th Circuit 2000

Whether a reasonable employee would feel compelled to resign depends on the facts of each case, but we consider the following factors relevant, singly or in combination: (1) demotion; (2) reduction in salary; (3) reduction in job responsibilities; (4) reassignment to menial or degrading work; (5) reassignment to work under a younger supervisor; (6) badgering, harassment, or humiliation by the employer calculated to encourage the employee's resignation...

Barrow v. New Orleans SS Ass'n, 10 F. 3d 292 - Court of Appeals, 5th Circuit 1994

A public employer who drove an employee having a contract of employment to resign by making life unbearable for him... might be violating the Fourteenth Amendment and section 1983. This would be a case of constructive discharge.

Brown v. Brienen, 722 F. 2d 360 - Court of Appeals, 7th Circuit 1983

A public employer obviously cannot avoid its constitutional obligation to provide due process by the simple expedient of forcing involuntary "resignations."

Stone v. University of Maryland Medical System Corp., 855 F. 2d 167 - Court of Appeals, 4th Circuit 1988

Congress meant to give a remedy to parties deprived of constitutional rights, privileges and immunities by an official's abuse of his position...the federal remedy under Section 1983 is supplementary to the state remedy and that the latter need not be first sought and refused before the federal one is invoked.

Monroe v. Pape, 365 US 167 - Supreme Court 1961

To state a claim against a municipality or a government official in his or her official capacity, a plaintiff must allege that a policy or custom of the government entity is responsible for the alleged constitutional violation.

Monell v. New York City Dept. of Social Servs., 436 US 658 - Supreme Court 1978

The law prohibits retaliatory work assignments that could well dissuade a reasonable worker from making or supporting a charge of discrimination.

Burlington N. & Sfr Co. v. White, 547 US - Supreme Court 2006

Sexual harassment that creates a hostile work environment is actionable as sex discrimination under Title VII... where such conduct has the purpose or effect of unreasonably interfering with an individual's work performance or creating an intimidating, hostile, or offensive working environment...Title VII affords employees the right to work in an environment free from discriminatory intimidation, ridicule, and insult...The plaintiff must show that the employer knew or should have known of the harassment, and took no effectual action to correct the situation.

Meritor Savings Bank, FSB v. Vinson, 477 US 57 - Supreme Court 1986

The law requires an employer to reasonably accommodate an employee's religion if it can do so without undue hardship.

Trans World Airlines, Inc. v. Hardison, 432 US 63 - Supreme Court 1977

Refusal to provide employment references in retaliation for filing complaint with EEOC could amount to a violation of Title VII.

Pantchenko v. CB Dolge Co., Inc., 581 F. 2d 1052 - Court of Appeals, 2nd Circuit 1978

On December 24, 1981, the District Court held that Brown had forfeited her right to pursue her claim under Title VII of the Civil Rights Act of 1964 because of her failure to file a complaint meeting the requirements of Rule 8 of the Federal Rules of Civil Procedure within 90 days of her receipt of the right-to-sue letter.

Baldwin County Welcome Center v. Brown, 466 US 147 - Supreme Court 1984

We believe that society and the policies underlying Title VII will be best served if, wherever possible, unlawful discrimination is attacked within the context of existing employment relationships.

Bourque v. Powell Elec. Mfg. Co., 617 F.2d 61 (5th Cir. 1980).

An employee is constructively discharged when his employer, rather than discharging him directly, intentionally creates a work atmosphere so intolerable that he is forced to quit involuntarily.

Terry v. Ashcroft, 336 F. 3d 128 - Court of Appeals, 2nd Circuit 2003

"Today, approximately 1 percent of all civil cases filed in federal court are resolved by trial."

Jeffrey Q. Smith and Grant R. MacQueen, "Going, Going, But Not Quite Gone". Judicature, Duke Law School Winter 2017 Volume 101 Number 4.